HOW OUR PARLIAMENT FUNCTIONS

An introduction to the Law, Practice and Procedure of the Parliament of Ghana

K.B. AYENSU • S.N. DARKWA

Sub-Saharan Publishers

This revised edition is published in Ghana in 2006 by
Sub-Saharan Publishers
P. O. Box LG 358
Legon, Accra

© Copyright text: K.B. Ayensu, S.N. Darkwa 2000

ISBN 9988- 550-88-X

Layout and cover design: Kwabena Agyepong

Printed in Mauritius by Book Printing Services Ltd

PREFACE

The first edition of this work was published thirty-five years ago. The author, K.B. Ayensu, first Clerk of Parliament of Independent Ghana, explained that the publication was meant to introduce Members to the law, practice and procedure of Parliament. Although the procedure at Westminster was our model, our rules and Standing Orders were adapted to suit our history and culture.

It has been said that an efficient and effective Parliament is not a static institution. Our Parliament has grown from One-Party State Parliament to a multi-party parliamentary democracy over the past three decades. Significant procedural reforms have evolved to reflect the changing needs.

K. B. Ayensu and I worked to update the first edition. The second edition is a near verbatim repeat of the first edition. The present edition seeks to update, clarify and extend some of the arguments of the first edition.

Members, officers and officials of Parliament at whom this edition is primarily aimed must come to full grips with the law, practice and procedure of Parliament to ensure the correctness of doing business in Parliament. Without the correct application of the rules and procedure, debate in Parliament can degenerate into a chaotic scene.

For the efficient operation of Parliament, the role of the Presiding Officer is crucial. He must be absolutely impartial in the Chair and must interpret the rules and the Standing Orders without fear or favour. He must protect the interest of all Members, particularly the Minorities, so that their frustrations may not find an outlet in walk outs. Indeed, trust in the Presiding Officer is the key to getting business through in the House.

The Clerk and his staff who are the principal advisers to the Presiding Officer and Members on procedural matters must be thoroughly grounded in the rules and procedures of the House. This calls for a thorough and constant training to upgrade their skills and broaden their outlook. They should at all times exhibit qualities of objectivity and impartiality in the application of the rules and procedures. They must remain apolitical so that the integrity of Parliament would remain unassailable in a multi-party democracy.

The public for whom Parliament exists must understand how the institution functions and what avenues are open to them to be involved in the legislative process. Because the decisions of Parliament affect every citizen, the Constitution has made provision for citizens to have opportunity to make public input into the making of laws to improve any legislative proposal called Bill. If citizens are required to meaningfully participate in the legislative process then the procedures of Parliament should not be shrouded in mystery; they must be comprehensible to the citizens. This edition attempts to simplify or explain the technical language used in Parliament for the benefit of legislators and non legislators.

S. N. Darkwa,
Accra

ACKNOWLEDGEMENTS

The first edition of this book was funded by the Danish International Development Assistance (DANIDA) Ghana, whose steadfast commitment to Ghana's democratic process and good governance is much appreciated.

The sudden demise of K. B. Ayensu, my co-author and mentor to whose memory the book is dedicated, dampened my spirit. It required an effort of will on my part to continue the work.

The Hon. Mr. Justice V .C. R. A. C. Crabbe, a renowned Parliamentary Draftsman, to the 1968 - 69 Constituent Assembly and Chairman or Speaker of the 1978 – 1979 Constituent Assembly that drafted the 1979 Constitution and H. E. Ole Blicher-Olsen, the Danish Ambassador were a source of encouragement to me. At the launch of our book *The Evolution of Parliament in Ghana* both Justice Crabbe and the Ambassador urged me to undertake and complete this work.

In spite of his heavy schedule as the Commissioner for Statute Law Revision, Justice Crabbe graciously spent his time to edit the book and made suggestions for its improvement. Ambassador Ole Blicher-Olsen took unusually keen interest in the project to enhance our democracy. I am greatly indebted to them.

Mr. Samuel Okyere, Administrative Officer, Evangel Assemblies of God Church and Ms. Linda Kwao, Private Secretary to the Commissioner diligently typed the manuscript.

SND
October, 2000.

FOREWORD TO THE THIRD EDITION

Since Ghana returned to a multi-party parliamentary democracy in 1993, Parliament has steadily evolved into a virile and lively institution. As it faces new challenges, its rules and procedures must be kept under constant review to make them relevant for development and progress.

Included in this edition is the topic: "How to exploit the procedural opportunities to advantage". We felt that the incidence of walkouts was rather unusually high in the second and third Parliaments of the Fourth Republic. As a disruptive tactic, walkouts must be rarely used as a last resort. We have underlined the importance of the committee system that could offer effective solutions to some of the weaknesses in our democratic process.

The public reception of the second edition exceeded our expectation. It has encouraged us to publish the third edition.

I wish to express deep appreciation to Ms Gwenn Ronyk, experienced and respected Clerk of the Legislative Assembly, Regina, Saskatchwen, Canada, who carefully edited the manuscripts. Ms Lovatt Monique, the Administrative assistant to the Clerk is particularly mentioned for her prompt delivery of the edited work.

I am indebted to Mr S.O. Dodoo, a former colleague and for many years, the Editor of our Parliamentary Debates, who provided the bulk of the material on the topic, *Hansard*. Mr. McJewells J. Annan, a Parliamentary staff diligently read the work in proof.

My special thanks to the Clerk to Parliament, Mr Ken Tachie who readily provided facilities for the transmission of the manuscripts. As usual, my former secretary, Ms Elizabeth Andzie Quainoe, diligently and speedily typed the manuscripts.

SND
October, 2003

TABLE OF CONTENTS

Chapter One

A BRIEF HISTORICAL BACKGROUND OF THE LEGISLATURE OF GHANA

Ghana was the first country in the sub-Saharan Africa and in the Commonwealth to achieve independence on 6th March, 1957. The political struggles that preceded this historic event date back over a hundred years.

Association with Sierra Leone and Lagos

Legislative power was first exercised in The Gold Coast in the reign of Queen Victoria(1837 – 1901). During the period 1850 – 1865, the Gold Coast, becoming for the first time a distinct dependency of the British Crown, was given its own Legislative Council. It consisted of the Governor and at least two other persons designated by Royal Instructions. It was required to make "as may from time to time be necessary for the peace, order and good government of our subjects and others within the said present or future forts and settlements in The Gold Coast, subject to rules and regulations made by Order in Council and to the right of the Crown to disallow any such ordinances, either in whole or in part, and with a saving for the future exercise of legislative power by Act of Parliament or Order in Council"

Laws passed by the Legislative Council were to be styled "Ordinances enacted by the Governor of our Forts and Settlements on the Gold Coast, with the Advice and Consent of the Legislative Council thereof" The Governor was required to withhold assent to any Ordinance which was repugnant to any Act of the British Parliament or to the Royal Charter or Royal Instructions, or which interfered with Christian worship, diminished public revenue, sanctioned the operation of lotteries, permitted divorce, etc. With a few exceptions an Ordinance did not come into effect until the pleasure of the Crown had been signified.

From 1866 to 1874 the Gold Coast was reunited with West African Settlements, and its Legislative Council was reduced in size. In 1874 the Gold Coast was again given a separate government. It was from then that the steady growth of the Legislature began, but even quite near the end of the 19th Century the powers of the Legislature were still limited and its area of authority undefined.

In 1888 the first African Unofficial Member was nominated to the Legislative Council. As time went on unofficial representation was increased but the European Official Members continued to be in the majority.

In 1916 the Legislative Council was reconstituted to include nine nominated unofficials, six of whom were Africans as opposed to eleven officials, and the Governor. The first Legislative Council elections ever to be held took place in 1925 under the Guggisberg Constitution. It was in this year that the practice of nominating mercantile and mining Members began. The Governor still retained complete control of legislation under the 1925 Constitution.

Under the 1946 Burns Constitution[1] which replaced the Guggisberg Constitution, the representatives of the people formed the majority in the Legislative Council and Ashanti was for the first time given representation.

The formation of the United Gold Coast Convention (UGCC) in 1947 and the Convention Peoples Party in 1949 created tremendous political awareness and the desire to assert the right of self-determination.

The Coussey Constitutional Committee
The political disturbances in February 1948 led to the appointment of the Watson Commission which recommended that the Burns Constitution of 1946 should be replaced with a Constitution in which African Ministers would be entrusted with the business of Government and accountable to an elected legislature. Following the recommendations of the Watson Commission, the Governor, Sir Gerald Creasy appointed a Constitutional Committee, the Coussey Committee whose chairman was Justice Henley Coussey (later Sir Henley) to examine proposals for constitutional and political reforms made in the Watson Report. The Coussey Report gave the Gold Coast a constitution under which a measure of self-government would be enjoyed. Dr. Kwame Nkrumah called that Constitution "bogus and fraudulent". It, however, formed the basis of the Legislative Assembly of 1951 which gave the Gold Coast limited responsible government.

In 1949 the Legislative Council was given jurisdiction over Southern Togoland under the United Kingdom Trusteeship. In 1951 the Legislative Assembly became the legislature of the Northern Territories also. Before these changes, the legislative jurisdiction over these areas resided exclusively in the Governor.

---

1. *It was described by Dr. J.B. Danquah as "outmoded at birth"*

In 1949 the Governor ceased to be ex-officio President of the Legislative Council and an unofficial Member was appointed President. This system continued until 1951 when the legislature elected its first Speaker. It was the beginning of representative government.

The first large-scale elections to the Legislative Assembly took place in 1951 when 75 Members were elected under the 1950 Constitution. In addition to that number there were nominated three ex-officio Members and six special Members representing commercial and mining interests. The Convention People's Party won the majority of seats, and Dr. Kwame Nkrumah was appointed Leader of Government Business.

The 1954 Amendment ushered in the era of responsible government

The 1957 [transitional] Constitution provided for an Assembly of a Speaker and 104 Members elected by political parties on the basis of universal adult suffrage. While the 1954 Constitution may be described as an advanced colonial legislature, at independence in 1957 the Constitution gave us a sovereign Parliament that was fashioned after the Westminster model.

In June, 1960 ten women were elected by the National Assembly to fill specially created seats. This was done under the Representation of the People (Women Members) Act, 1960. This action was taken to expose women to parliamentary life and if possible groom a few for responsible office, one of whom, later became a Minister. This system of election was not intended to be permanent. The Act made no provision for filling a vacancy caused by death, resignation or expulsion of a woman Member.

On 1st July, 1960 Ghana became a sovereign unitary Republic under the First Republican Constitution. On that day the National Assembly constituted under the Independence Constitution of 1957 became the First National Assembly of the First Republic with a new five-year lease of life.

In February, 1964 Ghana adopted a one-party system of government. A new Article inserted in the Constitution provided that,

(1)   In conformity with the interests, welfare and aspirations of the People and in order to develop the organisational initiative and the political activity of the People, there shall be one national party which shall be the vanguard of the People in their struggle to build a socialist society and which shall be the leading core of all organisations of the People.

(2)   The national party shall be the "Convention People's Party". [2]

The First National Assembly of the Republic was dissolved in May 1965 and a general election held in the following month in which all the 198 Members, all of them Members of the national party, the Convention People's Party, were returned unopposed. This number included 19 women. Before the election the electoral districts had been increased to 198 on the recommendation of the Delimitation Commission of 1964. The 1960 Constitution and the 1964 constitutional amendments conferred considerable powers and prerogatives on the President.

The National Assembly of 1965 came to an abrupt end on 24 February, 1966 when a coup d'etat overthrew the Nkrumah Government. The National Liberation Council (NLC) took the reins of government until under the 1969 Constitution, when it handed over to the Progress Party (PP) led by Dr. K.A. Busia who was elected Prime Minister after the general election on the 29th August 1969. Party politics was restored by the 1969 Constitution under which the National Assembly consisted of 140 Members elected on the basis of universal adult suffrage. The Convention People's party did not contest the election because it had been proscribed.

The Busia Government was overthrown by a coup d'état on 13th January, 1972. From then on the country was in the grip of four military governments: the National Redemption Council (NRC), the Supreme Military Council the First (SMC 1) from 1975 to 1978, The Supreme Military Council the Second (SMC 11) from 1978 to 4th June, 1979 and the Armed Forces Revolutionary Council (AFRC) from 4th June – September, 1979

In September 1979 the military government of the AFRC under much political pressure restored constitutional rule under the 1979 Constitution, the Third Republican Constitution. The People's National Party (PNP) won the general election held in June, 1979. The presidential election held in the same month, on the basis of universal adult suffrage, proved inconclusive and a run-off was held in July when Dr. Hilla Limann of the People's National Party (PNP) won against Mr. Victor Owusu, the Popular Front Party (PFP) presidential candidate.

The Armed Forces Revolutionary Council handed over power to the President–Elect on 24th September, 1979. Under the 1979 Constitution the President, Vice-President and Ministers of State and their deputies

---

2.   *1964 Constitutional Amendment to Republican Constitution of 1960*

were not Members of Parliament. The Constitution provided for a separation of powers between the Executive and Parliament. That was the first time Ghana moved away from the Westminster System. Parliament no longer consisted of the President and the Legislature, and the word "Parliament" was for the first time used to describe the Legislature only. Parliament had 140 seats. Its statutory life was five years.

On 31st December, 1981 the democratic government of the Third Republic was once more overthrown by a coup d'etat. Parliament was in abeyance until 1993 when Ghana once again returned to constitutional rule under the 1992 Constitution, the Fourth Republican Constitution, which provided for a hybrid system of government – a blend of parliamentary and presidential systems. The President, Vice President and some Ministers and Deputy Ministers were not Members of Parliament but have audience in Parliament. Ministers and Deputy Ministers were subject to parliamentary approval on their appointment.

Parliament had 200 members and a term of 4 years. The presidential election was won by Flt. Lt. J. J. Rawlings, Chairman of the Provisional National Defence Council (PNDC) who overthrew the government of President Dr. Hilla Limann. The New Patriotic Party (NPP) presidential candidate, Prof. Adu Boahen ran second. The minority parties boycotted the parliamentary elections because of the alleged irregularities in the presidential election which was held earlier.

The First Parliament of the Fourth Republic lived its full statutory life of four years. After the general elections in 1996 in which the National Democratic Congress presidential candidate, Flt. J.J. Rawlings won against the NPP presidential candidate, Mr. J.A. Kufour, the Second Parliament commenced its first sitting on 7th January, 1997 with a strong presence of 67 seats for the Minority Parties in Parliament.

The elections of 2000 marked a steady progress towards the consolidation of our democratic governance. The smooth transfer of power from a democratically elected government to another was significant. The prospect of such smooth transition had eluded Ghana for more than four decades after our Independence. It was, therefore, not surprising that the results of the elections were received with joyous celebrations throughout the country.

The achievement not only reinforced our passionate commitment to multiparty democracy. It also demonstrated our maturity and cohesion as a nation. The resilience and patience of the opposition that had waited for 30 years before gaining political power has much to commend it.

The government graciously conceded defeat and must be commended for ensuring peaceful transition.

The presidential election of 7th December, 2000 was inconclusive as none of the candidates received the required number of votes. The NPP Presidential Candidate, Mr. John Agyekum Kufuor and the National Democratic Congress Presidential Candidate, Prof. John Evans Atta Mills had to face a run-off on 28th December, 2000.

Mr. J.A. Kufuor was elected the 2nd President of the 4th Republic of Ghana in the run-off. The other parties opposed to the ruling government threw their weight behind the NPP which had earlier won the parliamentary election with 100 seats and the NDC with 92 seats. The People's National Convention (PNC) had 3 seats, the Convention People's Party 1 and Independent 4 seats. There were 19 Women.

Chapter Two

PURPOSE OF PROCEDURE

An institution of the nature of Parliament needs clearly defined procedures for the orderly conduct of its business. The business of Parliament is conducted in accordance with its procedures and rules – usually called the Standing Orders and an inherent jurisdiction often referred to as the "law, privileges, procedures and usages of Parliament". [3]

In the celebrated words of John Hatsell who was Clerk of the House of Commons for 52 years during the 18th century:

" ...there should be (for the purposes of procedure) a rule to go by, in order that there may be a uniformity of procedure in the business of the House not subject to the momentary caprice of the Speaker or the captious disputes of any of the Members, that order, decency and regularity, should be preserved in a large, numerous and consequentially sometimes tumultuous Assembly".[4]

Procedures are essential. They protect the rights of the minority against the majority who may wish to adopt measures without adhering to the rules and procedures of the House. They also protect the interests of the majority against the minority who may wish to frustrate the wishes of the majority by abusing the rules and procedures of the House. More importantly, they also protect the rights of the citizens against improper adoption of laws or measures. They are part of the rubric of orderly democratic government.

Standing Orders

The Constitution by article 110 authorises Parliament to make Standing Orders for the regulation and orderly conduct of its proceedings and the despatch of its business. The notice of a motion for the amendment of Standing Orders is accompanied by a draft of the proposed amendments. When the motion is moved and seconded it stands referred to the Standing Orders Committee and further proceedings are not taken on it until the Committee has reported to Parliament. The Speaker is the chairman of the Committee.

---

3. *Erskine May's Parliamentary Practice (21st Edition C. Boulton)*
4. *Hatsell, Precedents of Proceedings in the House of Commons*
   (1818 Edition Vol. 11)

SESSIONS, MEETINGS AND SITTINGS:

Session of Parliament

After a general election a new Parliament comes into being. The life of each Parliament is four years in accordance with article 113 (1) of the Constitution. During this period a number of sessions are held. The Constitution requires a new session to be held once at least in every year so that a period of twelve months should not elapse between the last Sitting in a Session and the first Sitting in the next. In practice a new session begins in January and continues for just under twelve months. But under article 113 of the Constitution, there is no Prorogation of Parliament.

Session is defined as the sittings of Parliament commencing when Parliament first meets after a prorogation or a dissolution and ending when Parliament is prorogued or dissolved without being prorogued.[5]

Prorogation is the act of closing a Session in anticipation of the commencement of another Session within the lifetime of the Parliament. The effect of prorogation is to suspend the power of the Parliament to transact business. Prorogation quashes all matters pending before Parliament. The period during which Parliament stands prorogued is called recess.[6]

Dissolution is the act of bringing to an end the life of the Parliament. On the dissolution of Parliament, Members of Parliament lose their mandates, their seats and their title. The Speaker and the Deputy Speakers however continue in office until immediately before the first Sitting of the new Parliament.

Before the 1979 and 1992 Constitutions, the summoning, prorogation and dissolution of the Parliament were the prerogatives of the President. In keeping with the doctrine of separation of powers between the Executive and Parliament, the President no longer has these prerogatives. At the end of its lifetime of four years Parliament automatically stands dissolved. But Parliament may extend its life after four years when Ghana is actually engaged in war for not more than twelve months at a time: article 113 (2) of the Constitution.

The Speaker exercises the power of summoning a new Session of Parliament by a Constitutional Instrument.

---

5. *Erskine May's p. 220*
6. *Standing Order No. 7 of the Parliament of Ghana*

Meetings

A Session is divided into periods called Meetings. A Meeting is defined as any sitting or sittings of Parliament commencing when Parliament first meets after being summoned at any time and terminating when Parliament is adjourned *sine die* or at the conclusion of the Session.

Adjournment

The period between the end of a Meeting and the commencement of the next Meeting held in the same session is known as an adjournment. Parliament is free to adjourn from day to day during the course of a Meeting and to adjourn sine die at the end of a Meeting.

Commencement of a Meeting

The date of the commencement of a Meeting is decided by the Speaker after consulting the leadership of the House. Not less than fourteen days before the date of a Meeting the Clerk gives notice in writing of the Meeting to each Member except when Parliament is adjourned to a specified date which is not more than fourteen days from the date of the adjournment.

Emergency Meetings

In cases of emergency, a meeting may be summoned on such shorter notice as the Speaker may determine. In this case the Clerk gives notification by a radio announcement. Article 113 (3) states that:

> *Where, after a dissolution of Parliament but before the holding of a general election, the President is satisfied that owing to the existence of war or of a state of Public emergency in Ghana or any part of Ghana, it is necessary to recall Parliament, the President shall cause to be summoned the Parliament that has been dissolved to meet.*

Sittings

A Meeting is made up of a number of Sittings. Sitting is defined as a period during which Parliament is sitting continuously without adjournment and a period during which it is in committee.[7] A suspension of proceedings during a sitting does not affect its category. A Sitting, unless the Speaker otherwise decides, commences at 10.00 a.m. The only exception is the Sitting with which a Session commences, the time

---

7. *Standing Orders – Interpretation*

for which is appointed by the Speaker by constitutional instrument in accordance with clause (1) of article 112 of the Constitution.

Unless Parliament has previously adjourned a Sitting ends at 2.00 p.m. or at such later time as the Speaker may decide. The Speaker may alter the date to which a Sitting has been adjourned during a Meeting after consulting the leadership of the House.

Oaths of Members

Members first take and subscribe before the Speaker the Oath of Allegiance and the Oath of a Member of Parliament as set out in the Second Schedule to the Constitution.

The Oath of Allegiance is as follows:

I ...do (in the name of the Almighty God swear) (solemnly affirm) that I will bear true faith and allegiance to the Republic of Ghana as by law established; that I will uphold the sovereignty and integrity of Ghana; and that I will preserve, protect and defend the Constitution of the Republic of Ghana (So help me God).

The Oath of a Member of Parliament is as follows:

I ...having been elected a Member of Parliament do (in the name of the Almighty God swear) (solemnly affirm) that I will bear true faith and allegiance to the Republic of Ghana as by law established; that I will uphold, protect and defend the Constitution of the Republic of Ghana; and that I will faithfully and conscientiously discharge the duties of a Member of Parliament. (So help me God).

Instead of taking the oath, a Member may make a solemn affirmation as prescribed by the Oaths Act.

Election of Speaker and Deputy Speakers

At the beginning of a new Parliament as a result of a dissolution, the House first meets for the election of a Speaker. Before Members proceed to the election of a Speaker they must ensure that there is a quorum. The person proposed as Speaker must have given his consent to be nominated.

Unlike most Parliaments, the Clerk acts as chairman to the House for the election.

A Member proposing a person to the House as its Speaker shall move a motion that such person "do take the Chair of this House as Speaker". The motion must be seconded without debate.

The Speaker is chosen by all Members, usually unopposed after consultation among Majority and Minority sides, to emphasise the cross-party nature of the choice. This non-partisan method of the choice of a Speaker is to ensure that the person who occupies the Chair is impartial.

But where more than one person is proposed a motion is moved and seconded in respect of each person and the House proceeds to elect a Speaker by secret ballot in accordance with the provisions of Standing Order No. 9.

A Member may, before taking the oaths, take part in the election of the Speaker. Until the Speaker has taken the Chair the Mace is not in evidence. When the Speaker-Elect has submitted to the will of the House the Speaker takes and subscribes the Speaker's Oath before the Chief Justice.

The Oath is as follows:

I ...do (in the name of the Almighty God swear) (solemnly affirm) that I will bear true faith and allegiance to the Republic of Ghana as by law established; that I will uphold the integrity of the Republic of Ghana; that I will faithfully and conscientiously discharge my duties as Speaker of Parliament; and that I will uphold, preserve, protect and defend the Constitution of the Republic of Ghana; and that I will do right to all manner of persons in accordance with the Constitution of Ghana and the laws and conventions of Parliament without fear or favour, affection or ill-will. (So help me God).

Speaker presides

When he has taken his oath the Speaker assumes the Chair. He gives a short acceptance speech and he is congratulated by the leadership of the House on his election. The Speaker presides in Parliament at all Sittings and in his absence a Deputy Speaker presides.

The Mace

Dismissing Parliament on the 20th of April, 1653, Cromwell said of the Mace, "What shall we do with this...? There, take it away." The Mace, the symbol of authority of Parliament, is entrusted to the Speaker. The daily Speaker's procession into the Chamber is led by the Marshal with the Mace signifying the ceremonial opening of each Sitting day in the House. The Marshal carries the Mace on his right shoulder and then places it in a special holder in front of the Clerk's Table where it remains throughout the Sitting as a symbol of the authority of Parliament.

When the Speaker is in the Chair, the Mace stands upright or perpendicular indicating the formal proceedings in the House. However, during the Consideration Stage of a Bill, the Mace is tilted towards the Chair indicating the informal nature of the proceedings. At this stage, the rules of debate are relaxed and Members can speak more than once to a question from the Chair.

The present Mace of Parliament was made when Ghana became a Republic in 1960. The upright position of the Mace in the Chamber may be likened to a linguist's staff of office; it also gives prominence to the head of the Mace which is the eagle, our heraldic bird.

The shaft of the Mace has six traditional stools symbolizing common sharing of responsibility, the presence of God in our society, lasting personality, prosperity, and presence and effect of feminine power in the society and pride.

The Adinkra symbols embossed between the stools denote the Omnipotence of God, Critical examination, Strength, Immortality, and Justice.

State opening of Parliament

On the first day of a Session,[8] the President, in obedience to article 67 of the Constitution, attends Parliament in person to perform a most important function, that of turning the wheel to set in motion the machine of the Session. At this Sitting he delivers the Sessional Address in which he tells Parliament about the policies which the Government proposes to follow during the Session – "a message on the State of the Nation".

The ceremony that attends the opening of Parliament is one of pomp and pageantry. Shortly after taking the Chair the Speaker goes out of the chamber to meet the President whose arrival is heralded by *fontom-*

---

8. *A subsequent day in the case of the first session of a new Parliament.*

from[9]. The President drives in state to Parliament House escorted by a motorcade and then by a cavalcade. He inspects a guard of honour. Having been received by the Speaker and the Leader of the House in the central lobby, he enters the chamber to the sound of *mmenson*[10]. He is conducted by the Speaker's procession and is immediately preceded by the bearer of the sword of state. He is accompanied by Army, Naval and Air Force aides and ten linguists representing the ten Regions of Ghana.

Parliament made an innovation to this old convention that requires the President to formally open a new session of Parliament. In the second and third sessions of the third Parliament the Speaker formally opened Parliament. The Sessional Address by the President followed a couple of weeks later in both cases. This change of convention may be seen as Parliament asserting its independence of the Executive.

Sword of State

During the presence of the President in the House, the Sword of State, usually regarded as the symbol of authority of the President, takes the place of the Mace.

Sessional Address

At the beginning of each Session of Parliament and before the dissolution of Parliament the President is required by article 67 of the Constitution to deliver to Parliament a message on the State of the Nation. The address given by the President at the beginning of a session is normally called the Sessional Address and may be debated.

---

9. *A set of drums of State.*
10. *The seven horns of the State.*

Chapter Three

BUSINESS OF PARLIAMENT

The Business of Parliament is of two kinds: Government Business and Private Members' Business.

Government Business

Government Business comprises the items of business initiated by the Government in Parliament. The items include Government sponsored Bills, Motions and Ministerial Statements, Papers laid on the Table and Resolutions. In addition to these and others, an item of business initiated by a Private Member but taken up in Government-allotted time may be called a government business.

Private Members' business

Private Members' business includes Bills and Motions initiated by Private Members and statements made by them. Private Members may also bring into the House for discussion matters of urgent public importance, move a motion to thank the President for the Sessional Address, ask Questions of Ministers, raise questions of Privileges and so on. Bills and Motions introduced by Members are usually called Private Members' Bills and Private Members' Motions.

Order of business

Standing Order No. 53 provides the order in which the business for each Sitting shall be taken. The items include:

(a) Prayers
(b) Oaths
(c) Address by the President
(d) Messages from the President
(e) Formal Communications
(f) Questions to Ministers

Business Statement

The Business of the House is determined by the Business Committee of which the Majority Leader and Minister for Parliamentary Affairs is the chairman. The business for the whole week is determined in advance by the Business Committee which also arranges the order of items to be taken on a particular day. Every Friday the chairman of the Committee announces the business to be taken the following week in his weekly business statement. But when the first week of a Meeting commences on a day earlier than Friday, he makes a statement of the business arranged for the remainder of the week.

Prayers
A Sitting begins with two prayers read by the Speaker. After prayers the Speaker must satisfy himself that a quorum is present before he says "Order, Order" to commence the day's proceedings.

Commencement of proceedings
Commencement of proceedings comes under two headings:
    (a) BEFORE THE COMMENCEMENT OF
        PUBLIC BUSINESS; and

    (b) AT THE COMMENCEMENT OF
        PUBLIC BUSINESS.

By public business is meant Bills and motions initiated by the Government in the House. Before the commencement of public business the items that may be taken are oaths, Address by the President, Messages from the President, Speaker's Announcements, elections of Deputy Speakers, Presentation of Papers, Petitions, Questions, Statements by Ministers, complaints of contempt of Parliament, Personal Statements, Presentation of Government Bills and Motions and Motions for the introduction of Private Members' Bills.

Parliamentary Working Papers

Order Paper, Votes and Proceedings and Hansard - Official Report
A fundamental rule of debate in Parliament is that notice must be given in advance before a motion or an amendment can be moved. This means that no business, except in urgent circumstances, should be sprung on the House for debate. In practice, every item of business to be considered must be handed in at the Table Office so that it may be printed or published and made available to Members for the day of debate. Before the Parliamentary business starts, each Member is provided with a daily bundle of printed papers called the '**Vote**'. The most important paper in the vote is the **Order Paper**.

    The **Order Paper** gives the various items of business of the day accompanied by a Provisional Order Paper for the next sitting. In effect, the Order Paper is the daily agenda for the business to be done in the

Chamber and sometimes in Committee sittings outside the Chamber. Although the items of business are given in chronological order, by leave of the Speaker, the order of business as set out in the Order Paper may be varied when the Speaker is satisfied that there are sufficient grounds for the variation.

There are also three important documents included in the Vote everyday. These are the *Votes and Proceedings*, the *Hansard* (– the Official Report) and the Notice Paper.

The Votes and Proceedings are the official record of *res gestae*, that is, the things done and decided in the Chamber. For example, the three readings of a Bill and the formal decisions taken on motions and transactions and other business of the House are recorded in this publication. Also included in the Votes and Proceedings are the list of Members in attendance at a sitting of the House, the Questions asked and answered, reports from Committees without the actual proceedings, and Statements by Ministers and Members. They, however, do not record the things said in the Chamber. The *Votes and Proceedings* are compiled by the Clerks at the Table and signed by the Presiding Officer and the Clerk of the House.

Points of order concerning the accuracy of the *Votes and Proceedings* may be raised at the time appointed for Personal Statements.

The *Notice Paper* contains notices of Questions and Motions as well as proposed amendments to a Bill tabled on a previous day.

Another important printed document that is available to the Speaker, Members and Senior Officers is the *Hansard* or the Official Report of Debates of Parliament. The *Hansard* is fully treated in chapter seven.

Precedence regarding business
Government business has precedence over Private Members' business, unless the House decides otherwise. The days allotted for Government business are Tuesdays, Wednesdays, and Thursdays, and Government is free to arrange its business as it wishes.

Private Member's Day
Friday is Private Members' Day. On that day Private Members' business has precedence over Government business. However, the Business Committee can put down Government Business on a Friday before Private Members' business if there is good reason to do so.

Ballot for Private Members' Business
Private Members may also be given time to initiate business during Government time. Examples of such business are Questions and adjournment motions. Private Members' motions, Private Members' Bills and half-hour motions are placed on the Order Paper in an order determined by a ballot. Private Members have the opportunity to participate in all activities including Government Business and the Business of the House.

The Vice-President, or a Minister or Deputy Minister who is not a Member of Parliament may attend a Sitting and participate in the proceedings but without the right to vote.

Language
The proceedings of Parliament are ordinarily conducted in the English language, but a Member may exercise the option to address the House in one of the major languages if it is accompanied by an English translation. It is permissible for a Member to use an expression in another language provided he accompanies it with an English translation.

Presiding in the Chamber
The Speaker presides over the proceedings in Parliament. He is at liberty, without announcement, to ask one of the Deputy Speakers to take the Chair who then is invested with all the powers of the Speaker until the Speaker is again able to take the Chair. The Speaker remains in the Chair during Question time, ministerial statements and other main business for the day. During major debates, and difficult situations he may not leave until the front bench spokespersons from both sides have spoken.

If the Speaker and both Deputy Speakers are absent the House upon a motion elects a Member, who is not a Minister, then present to take the Chair. The Member exercises all the powers of the Speaker for that Sitting only.

Laying of Papers

A Paper may be presented to Parliament only by the Speaker, a Minister, or the Chairman of a Committee. Upon the Speaker announcing "Papers for Presentation" a Paper, of which copies have been distributed to Members, is deemed to have been laid on the Table. Where there has not been a distribution a copy of the Paper must be laid physically on the Table. The person presenting a Paper may, if he so desires, make a short explanatory statement upon its presentation.

Personal statements

By the indulgence of the House and the leave of the Speaker, a Member may at the appropriate time explain a matter of a personal nature or make a statement on a matter of urgent public importance. The terms of the proposed statement should first be submitted to the Speaker. A statement, other than personal statement, may be commented upon by other Members.

Correction of Votes and Proceedings

Points of order concerning the accuracy of the Votes and Proceedings, the official record of proceedings and the official report commonly known as Hansard may be raised at the time appointed for Personal Statements. A Member may suggest corrections to the transcript of his speech before the Official Report is printed but the corrections must be confined to verbal corrections such as grammar, vocabulary and construction.

Chapter Four

FUNCTIONS OF PARLIAMENT

The main functions of Parliament may conveniently be divided into three: Deliberative, Legislative and Voting of Supply[11] otherwise called the financial function.

DELIBERATIVE FUNCTION

Parliamentary control of government

A democratic government must be held accountable for its actions to Parliament. The effectiveness of Parliament must therefore be judged by the extent to which it exercises its oversight responsibilities over the government or the Ministers and the Public Services. It has been said that the price of democracy is eternal scrutiny[12]. To be able to effectively scrutinize government activities and policies the Parliament must have the means to practise this vigilance. Two common means of holding the Government to account are either to move a motion, or to ask Questions of Ministers. In whatever business Parliament is engaged, Members debate issues before determining the question before them. Deliberation arises when a motion is moved and seconded. This is what is called the Deliberative or Inquiry function. The inquiry or investigative role of Parliament may be exercised through Motions or Questions raised in the House.

Motions

The deliberative function, sometimes called the function of criticism, is exercised in the main by substantive motions which lead to debate. Motion is a generic term covering all proposals submitted to the House for its decision. A motion is the expression of the opinion or wish of one or more than one Member which is put before the House. If the House accepts it, it becomes the opinion or the will of the whole House.

Substantive motion, Amendments

Motions are primarily of two classes: dependent and independent. A substantive motion belongs to the class of independent motions. It may be defined as a self-contained proposal which is framed in such a way as to be capable of being closely debated and expressing the opinion or

---

11. *That is money*
12. *JAC Griffith and M. Ryle - Parliament, functions, practice and procedures p. 16*

will of the House.It is called "substantive" because it has "substance", a definite subject matter for debate. Amendments are dependent motion because their very being is dependent on the existence of a substantive motion. See page 27 where Amendments are dealt with.

Debate
Debate is the method by which the House passes laws and resolutions, issues orders and makes known its opinions and its will. The process of debate begins when a Member moves a motion of which the Member has given notice. The Member rises when called and says: "Mr. Speaker, I beg to move, That... the Member then supports the motion with a speech although it is not essential that the Member should make one, and ends by saying: "Mr. Speaker I beg to move." A private Member's motion must always be moved by the Member who has given notice of it unless it is in the name of the chairman of a Committee. A Government motion may be moved by a Minister.

Seconding of motions
A motion is seconded with the formula: "Mr. Speaker, I beg to second the motion". A speech is not essential. Where a speech is not made, the Member seconding the motion retains the right to speak to the question at a later stage of the debate. A Government motion need not be seconded. After a motion has been seconded the Speaker gives the House possession of it by proposing the question. To do this the Speaker says: "The motion as moved (and seconded) is for the consideration of the House".

Winding up, reply for Government
When as many Members as possible have expressed their views on the question, the proposer or some other Member on behalf of the proposer winds up the debate. In the case of a private Member's motion, the Minister responsible for the subject of the debate (or another Minister in that behalf) replies for the Government before the debate is wound up.

Deciding motions
The Speaker then puts the question, that is, recites the terms of the motion and invites those in favour of the motion and those against it to indicate by saying Aye or No. When the voices die down the Speaker says "The question is, That..." (or, where the terms of the motion are lengthy, "That the motion be agreed to") The Speaker then adds "As

many as are in favour say Aye; as many as are not in favour say No. I think the Ayes (or Noes) have it." The Speaker ends this colloquy by confirming with the "The Ayes (or Noes) have it."

Simple majority, equality of votes: original and casting vote

Unless it is otherwise provided all questions brought before the House are determined by a majority of the votes of the Members present and voting. If the votes of the Members are equally divided the motion is considered lost. The Speaker has neither an original nor a casting vote. A Member presiding has an original but no casting vote.

Division

When a motion has been decided by means of collecting voices Aye and No, the Speaker's decision may be challenged by a Member claiming a division. The real purpose of a division is to have on record the names of Members voting for and against a motion.

When the Speaker grants a division, two tellers take their places in each of the division lobbies. As Members file through the lobbies they are counted by the tellers and their names are recorded by the division clerks. Unlike in other countries, the tellers may vote.

Counting Members

The Speaker may refuse the claim for a division where the Speaker considers the case to be frivolous, and instead ask the Clerk to count the number of Members for and against the motion.

Order and resolution

A motion, when agreed to, results either in an order or in a resolution of the House. It results in an order if it directs a Committee or Members or Officers of Parliament, or the order of its own proceedings or the acts of persons whom the proceedings concern. It results in a resolution if it declares the opinions and purposes of the House. An Order of the House is meant to be carried out by those whom it directs. A resolution of the House does not bind anybody. It may be helpful to observe the distinction between an order and a resolution – the latter is usually employed erroneously to describe both.

Withdrawal of motions

A Member who has proposed a motion may withdraw it but if the question has already been proposed, that is, if the House has already been given possession of the motion, the Member may do so only by leave of the majority of Members present. To ascertain whether the House is willing to grant leave, the Speaker says, "Is it the pleasure of the House that leave be given to the Member to withdraw this motion?" The matter is determined in the usual way, that is by the collection of voices (voice vote).

RULES OF DEBATE
As the rules governing the conduct of debate are many the most important ones will be dealt with.

Quorum
A business which is not an adjournment may not be transacted in the House if a Member brings to the notice of the Chair the fact that there are less than one-third of the Members present, excluding the Member presiding. After proceedings have begun the Chair cannot personally take objection that there is no quorum.

A quorum of one-third of all the Members present is required to commence business in the House.[13] A quorum of one-half of the Members present is required to approve loan agreements, or decide on motions before the House.[14] With regard to constitutional amendments, it will require two-thirds of all the Members to approve the proposed amendments.[15] Until the Second Republic, decisions on a matter before the House could be taken by one-third of the Members present. It was felt that as decisions and Acts of Parliament affect all citizens at least one-half of all the Members present should take those decisions.

Addressing the House
A Member may address the House only when the Member is called by the Speaker. He must speak from his place unless he is a Member entitled to the front bench, in which case he may speak from the despatch box. A Member may only address the Speaker; in other words, in his speech the second person "you" must be used only in relation to the Speaker. A Member may not say "Mr. Speaker and Members of this honourable House". He should refer to Members in the third person with phrases like "the Majority or Minority Leader of the House", "the Member for Offinso North," "the Member who has just spoken". A Minister should refer to another Minister as "my colleague, the Minister of…".

---

13. Article 102 of the Constitution
14. Articles 104, 181 of the Constitution
15. Article 291 (3) of the Constitution

Reading speeches

A Member may not read his speech, but this rule is relaxed for Ministers and for Members making their maiden speeches. A Member may, however, refresh his memory from his notes. In order not to defeat this rather good rule one should endeavour to draw the line between reading one's speech and refreshing one's memory from notes.

Interruption of speeches

A Member who has the floor must not be interrupted by another Member unless the Member speaking yields to him, or the Member wishing to interrupt rises to a point of order.

Point of order

A Member rises to a point of order when he desires to bring to the notice of the House the fact that a trespass has been committed against a rule. If a Member wishes to interrupt the speech of a Member who has the floor but has no point of order to raise to, he should find some ingenious method to attract the attention of the Member speaking. If he succeeds in doing so the Member speaking may yield to him. If a Minister wishes to interrupt a speech he should adopt the same procedure.

A Member normally yields to a Minister out of courtesy. If a Member gets the opportunity to interrupt a speech but does not have a point of order to raise, he should not preface his statement with peculiar phrases like "on a point of explanation" and "on a point of information".

Points of order are raised with respect to a departure from the Standing Order or procedure in practice during debate in the House or Committee business.

Interruption of Debate

A Member has the right to stand in his place to interrupt debate by drawing attention to the Chair on a point of order to what he considers to be an infringement of the rule if the Chair has not perceived that breach.

Debates may be interrupted,

(a) by a point of order being raised;
(b) by a matter of privilege suddenly arising;
(c) by attention being called to absence of a quorum; and
(d) by attention being called to the presence of strangers in the Chamber.

Offensive words

It is out of order to use offensive or blasphemous or unbecoming words or to impute improper motives to any other Member or to make personal allusions. Personal attacks on persons outside the House must not be indulged in, but such attacks must not be confused with criticism in respect of public duties. Allegations made in good faith are quite permissible but it is first a requisite that the Member making them satisfies himself regarding the authenticity of the information.

Unparliamentary language

Members' decorum must be reflected in their choice of words, that is to say, their language must never be unparliamentary, even during moments of great heat. Various words have been ruled as unparliamentary. They include "lie", "hypocrite". In the heat of debate during the First Republic, the Member for Amansie East, Joe Appiah told the Minister of Finance K. A. Gbedemah that he lied to the House when the Minister claimed that the Paper in his hand was a White Paper to support his argument instead of a Green Paper.

Mr. Speaker ruled that the word "lied" was unparliamentary. The Member then withdrew the word and said that the "Minister preferred expediency to truth". Another example. In the House of Commons, Mr. Disraeli accused the Government that "half the Cabinet are asses". On being asked by the Speaker to withdraw this remark he said that "half the Cabinet are not asses".[16] However, heated language in certain circumstances may be understood or overlooked.

Substantive motion on conduct of Speaker, Member of Parliament, Chief Justice

The conduct of the Speaker, Members of Parliament, the Chief Justice, the Justices of the Superior Court of Judicature and other persons engaged in the administration of justice may not be raised, except upon a substantive motion. In other words, it is out of order to raise the conduct of any of these persons unless a substantive motion dealing with that person is before the House.

Matters sub judice

Reference should not be made to a matter to which judicial decision is pending in a way that may prejudice the interests of parties to that matter. The Speaker is the judge of what is sub judice and what is not. Here

---

16. *Derek Heater: Parliament at work*

again he should be indulgent if the Member he has ruled out of order commences an argument.

Relevance
A Member must always speak to the question, that is, he must not introduce matters outside the scope of the question proposed from the Chair. As it is not always easy to decide what is relevant and what is not, the Chair should indulge a Member who has been ruled out of order if he attempts to advance arguments to prove that the statement to which objection has been taken is relevant. Irrelevance in debate or undue prolongation of speech (a term for filibustering) may be ruled out of order.

Out of order Motions, Bills.
It is said that Parliament can debate any motion. But it is out of order to admit for debate certain motions that the Constitution does not allow. For example, it is out of order to introduce a motion to turn Ghana into a one-party state[17] or to introduce a retroactive legislation in Parliament.[18]

Also motions and Bills that have been dealt with in a session cannot be brought before the House in that same session![9] Motions that are unduly long are not allowed (they should not exceed 250 words).[20] Motions which anticipate a matter already due to be considered in a reasonably near future will be disallowed for debate.

The rules also apply to admissibility of Questions that may be asked of Ministers in the House.

Misbehaviour
If a Member misbehaves during a debate there is ample provision for dealing with him in an appropriate manner.[21] This ranges from a direction for discontinuance of his speech to suspension from the service of the House for a specified period.

Motion not to hear Member
The motion, that a Member be no longer heard, may only be moved where a Member has used objectionable words and on being called to order has failed to retract or explain such words and offer an apology

---

17. *Article 3 (1) of the Constitution*
18. *Article 107 of the Constitution*
19. *Erskine May's Parliamentary Practice p.326*
20. *Erskine May's Parliamentary Practice p.125*
21. *Standing Order No. 100*

to the satisfaction of the Speaker. The question on such a motion is put without amendment or debate.

Half Hour Motions

Another method of exercising the deliberative function is by moving a half hour motion. A half hour motion is a substantive motion which is not calculated to attract full-dress debate. On the day on which the order paper contains the item half hour motion, the Speaker interrupts business half an hour before the time for adjournment of the House and calls upon the Member in whose name the item stands. Now that the House may adjourn for such period beyond the normal closing hour as the Speaker may decide, the half hour motion is merely the last item of business to be taken. In any case the proceedings must not exceed thirty minutes. Only one such motion may be taken at a Sitting.

The Minister responsible for the matter raised in the half hour motion may briefly respond to the issue. As has been stated earlier, motions are either dependent or independent. The two types of motions that have been dealt with – the ordinary substantive motion and the half hour motion – belong to the independent class.

Superseding Motions

In the class of dependent motions are Superseding motions. Superseding motions consist of dilatory motions and the previous question.

Dilatory Motions

A dilatory motion may be described as a motion proposed with the aim of delaying the decision on a question already proposed from the Chair. During a debate a Member may move, "That this House do now adjourn" or, "That the debate be now adjourned". If that motion is accepted by the Speaker he proposes it as a new question, and the new question supersedes the original question.

Previous Question

The object of the previous question is to withhold from the decision of the House a question that has already been proposed from the Chair. A Member may move "That the question be not now put".

An interesting feature of the previous question is that if it is negatived, the question on the original motion is put forthwith.

Closure of Debate

If after a question has been proposed a Member moves, "That the question be now put", the Speaker is bound to put the question forthwith, which must be decided without amendment or debate, unless he considers that the motion is an abuse of the rules of the House or an infringement of the rights of the minority. When the motion has been agreed to and the matter consequent on it has been decided, a Member may move that any other question already proposed from the Chair be now put.

If the Chair is willing the question is put forthwith and decided without amendment or debate. The closure can only be moved when the Speaker is himself in the Chair. For a motion for the closure to succeed it must be supported by a majority of Members.

Amendments

An amendment may be described as a motion which is proposed with the aim of altering the terms of a question before the House. Its object may be either to modify the question and thus make it more acceptable, or to present a different proposition as an alternative to the question before the House. An amendment may take one or three forms:

(a) a proposition to delete words;

(b) a proposition to insert words;

(c) a proposition to delete words and to insert other words instead.

It is possible to propose an amendment to an amendment. In such a case the second amendment becomes subsidiary to the first and must be disposed of first.

Deleting words

Upon an amendment to delete any of the words of a motion the Speaker proposes the question by saying, "The question is, that the words '...' be deleted from the question". Upon an amendment to insert words in, or add words at the end of a motion the Speaker proposes the question by saying, " The question is, That the words '...' be there inserted (or added)". Upon an amendment to delete words and insert (or add) other words instead, the Speaker first says "The question is that the words '...'be deleted from the question" and if the question is agreed to, he says, "The question is, That the words '...' be there inserted (or added)". If the question is negatived, no further amendment may be proposed to the words the deletion of which the House has not agreed to.

USING PROCEDURAL OPPORTUNITIES TO ADVANTAGE

Walkouts from the Chamber not desirable tactics

The incidence of walkouts from the Chamber during debates was rather unusually high in the Second and Third Parliaments of the Fourth Republic. The Minority side in the Second Parliament resorted to walkouts to express their frustrations at some of the rulings from the Chair.

With the reversal of roles in the Third Parliament, the Minority side (who were in majority in the Second Parliament) also adopted this tit for tat tactic to register their disappointment at some of the rulings from the Chair. This disruptive tactic must be rarely used as a last resort to draw public attention. The public may be interested in the quality of debates and alternative programmes or policies to enable them make a choice of government in the next elections. Therefore walkouts will not shed favourable light on the parties that employ these tactics.

Procedural options provide balanced opportunity

The procedural devices available to both sides of the House are sufficient to provide a balanced opportunity to ensure smooth flow of business in the House. It is the responsibility of the government, or the Majority side, to declare and justify its policies, defend them in debate, and have a reasonable opportunity to get its legislative programme passed by the House.

It is the duty of the Minority side to force full disclosure of such policies, seek explanations, and record its dissent and the reasons for it, and offer alternative policies.

The procedures of the House are intended to protect the interest of Minority side thus allowing the Minority to have its say and the Majority to have its way.

Procedural opportunities available to the Minority

Looking closely at the rules, we may find that if the Minority does not like a particular measure of law proposed by the government it can use procedural devices to obstruct government business.

Some of the disruptive opportunities available to the Minority include making of lengthy but relevant speeches so that debate will be prolonged to the extent that supporters on the government side may not stay the course; raising many points of order each of which has to be ruled on by a patient Speaker.

The other obstructive tactic is the use of calling for a lack of quorum to disrupt parliamentary proceedings.

Procedural opportunities available to Government
On the other hand, there are procedural measures available to the Majority or government to ensure passage of its business – motions, resolutions and bills – through the House.

The procedural devices to prevent obstruction of parliamentary business so that deliberations are not unduly protracted include:
  (a) Debate must be relevant to the question proposed by the Chair – i.e. the motion.
  (b) Forbidding Members to indulge in "tedious repetition" of arguments already advanced.
  (c) Members must speak only once to a motion being debated and must not read their speeches: Motions must not re-open matters already decided during the same session, except on a substantive motion for rescission.

Other methods to ensure taking of decisions after a motion has been sufficiently debated include:

  (a) **"Closure"** - Any member may move **"that the question be now put"**. When this motion has been moved the presiding officer must instantly decide whether a closure of debate is justified. He need not provide reasons for his decision. The House will immediately proceed to vote on the motion if the Speaker allows it.
  (b) '**The previous question**' - The motion is the opposite of '**closure motion**'. The 'previous question' motion is "That the question be not now put". If this motion is agreed to the original question or motion cannot be put. But if the 'previous question' motion is **negatived** the original motion is put.
  (c) '**quillotine**' – This is an allocation of time order for debate. Within the time allotted for debate, there is no room for obstructive motions or other business.

Both sides must be heard in debate
In the eyes of Members of Parliament, the most important job of the presiding officer is to balance the rights of the minorities or those who hold different views from the majority. The procedure and practices of the House provide balanced opportunity for both Majority and Minority sides to be heard in order to ensure smooth flow of business.

In this connection, the Minority must be given a reasonable chance to oppose the government, that is, the Minority must have its say while the government or Majority must have a reasonable opportunity to get its legislative programme through the House. Consultation and co-operation between the Majority and the Minority through what is generally called the "usual channels" ensures smooth running of parliamentary business. Disruptive tactics such as walkouts must be used as a last resort.

QUESTIONS

Questions to Ministers
The third method of carrying out the deliberative function is by addressing Questions to Ministers. Although the obvious purpose of a Question is to seek information, most Questions are in fact asked with the intention of pressing for action or ventilating grievances. Questions must be confined to public affairs for which Ministers are officially responsible. A Minister is required to respond to a question within twenty-one days on receipt of the question.

Questions regarding statutory bodies
Questions relating to matters which are under the control of a statutory body are restricted to those matters for which a Minister has been made responsible by law or which affect the general policy of that body. In exceptional cases, where the Speaker considers the matter to be of sufficient public importance, he may allow Questions relating to matters of day-to-day administration of a statutory body.

It is felt that statutory bodies, especially those of an industrial or commercial character, should not be subjected to the full rigours of parliamentary democracy.

Notice requested, urgent Questions
Notice of intention to ask a Question is given by delivering the Question in writing to the Office of the Clerk at least ten days before the day on which it is proposed to ask the Question. A Question may be asked without notice only if it is of an urgent character relating either to a matter of public importance or the arrangement of parliamentary business, and the leave of the Speaker has been obtained. The Member's name must be written on the copy so delivered.

Questions for oral answers
If an oral answer is desired the Question should be marked with an asterik. The answer to a Question not so marked is communicated in writing and printed in the Official Report.

Conditions
Among the basic rules concerning the form and content of questions are,
  (a) a Question should not contain arguments;
  (b) it must have a factual basis;

(c) it should avoid personal allusions;

(d) it must relate to matters for which a Minister is responsible;

(e) it should not refer to a matter which is sub judice.

The Speaker is the final authority as to the adminisibility or otherwise of a Question.

Form of notice

Notice of a Question must be given in the indirect form. For example, "Mr.AB: to ask the Minister of Foreign Affairs, if an embassy will be opened in Utopiana". For purposes of uniformity a Question of a purely interrogatory nature should begin with "whether" and a Question requesting action with "if". In the above example, Mr. AB has made a request. If he intended his Question to be purely interrogatory it would have read: "To ask the Minister of Foreign Affairs, whether an embassy will be opened in Utopiana".

Supplementary Question

When a Question has been answered orally in the House a supplementary Question may be put by a Member without notice, for the further elucidation of a matter of fact regarding which the answer has been given. A supplementary Question must not be used to introduce matters not included in the original Question.

Question time is the most lively feature of Parliamentary proceedings. It is one of the best methods of keeping Ministers on their toes to the extent that sometimes, embarrasing admissions are made by Ministers when supplementary Questions are asked.

We reproduce from the Hansard of 11th March 1971 a question asked of the Minister of Foreign Affairs which was answered.

FOREIGN AFFAIRS
Sale of military helicopters to
South Africa

"**Dr. Obed Asamoah:** asked the Minister of Foreign Affairs whether and under what circumstances does the Government of Ghana contemplate unilateral action against the United Kingdom for the unwarranted sale of mllitary helicopters to South Africa in defiance of

African opinion and in contravention of the United Nations Resolutions.

Minister of Foreign Affairs (Mr. William Ofori Atta): Mr. Speaker, first of all, may I apologise to you and the House that when this question was to be put, I was not in the House, I was in the precincts of the House consulting with the Clerk over one or two relevant matters. I apologise sincerely for not being in the House. Members opposite, especially the man with the bald head, know I was here [*Laughter*]

The Leader of the Opposition has commanded me to specify which of the bald-headed men I am talking of. If I may say so, the gentleman directly opposite me.

Mr. Alex Hutton-Mills: I can only say that the Minister is suffering from an optical illusion [*Laughter.*]

Mr. William Ofori Atta: There are several degrees of "ways". We have the "feeder road" and the "motorway". I answer as follows: In the statement issued by the Government on Tuesday, on February 23, on the British Government's decision to sell arms to South Africa, it was stated that the Government of Ghana "is also consulting sister African countries and other members of the Commonwealth for any concerted action which may be deemed necessary". These consultations are still continuing. Any further action by the Government will be determined by the outcome of those consultations.

Dr. Asamoah: Does the Minister think that it is reasonable to expect concerted action from sister African States in view of the following facts:

(1) the approval of the sale of arms by Britain to South Africa by a sister country like Malawi;

(2) the impasse over the representation of General Amin's Government in the organisation of African Unity; and

(3) the condoning of the sale of French arms to South Afiica by so many French African States.

9.20 a.m.

Mr. William Ofori Atta: I thank the hon. Member for listing all these difficulties. The Government does not envisage that the action should be universal; that we are going to have unanimity - all members agreeing before we take a concerted action. In spite of these differences of opinion with one, two, three or even four African states, we still believe the effectiveness of our action will depend on the number of people who are doing practically the same thing; and if we are to take any unilateral action it will be after we have made consultations.

Dr. Obed Asamoah: Does the Minister know that before the intention to sell arms was announced by the British Government certain statements or expressions of intention had been made by the Government of Ghana that Britain would be expelled from the Commonwealth if such arms were sold; and if he is aware, is he aware that such intentions were not made conditional upon consultations now with other African countries?

Mr. William Ofori Atta: I regret to say that the hon. Member is wrong. The statement said that if any such action should be taken by the British Government the Ghana Government would consult with others to take a concerted action, not excluding the possibility of expelling Britain from the Commonwealth.

Mr. S. K. Osei-Nyame: Will the Minister inform this House at what level these consultations are taking place and how soon he expects the consultations to be completed in view of the fact that the Minister himself does not appear to be involved in these consultations.

Mr. William Ofori Atta: The Minister and, in fact, the Government are involved in these consultations. The other countries are also sovereign states, and we cannot determine the time for them, but we are making consultations with Commonwealth countries, the Organization of African Unity members, and even we have instructed our Permanent Representative in the United Nations to consult with other members of like mind.

Dr. Asamoah: Will the Minister give assurance to this House that if the consultation that the Government is carrying out should not yield any concerted action, the Government will be prepared to take unilateral action against Britain over the sale of arms to South Africa.

Mr. William Ofori Atta: This House is fully aware that the Progress Party Government is a very wise government and that after consultations if it has to take any action it will be a very wise action.

Dr. Asamoah: If I may seek the guidance of the Chair. I think the Minister has not answered my question. He said that if there is no concerted action, if the Ghana Government should take any action, it will be a wise action. 1 want an assurance from the Minister that the Government will take unilateral action if the consultations are not successful. We do not want these conditional statements.

Mr. William Ofori Atta: The purpose of any action of the Government must be towards an effective end. This Government will not, for the sake of brinkmanship or showmanship, do anything which will not be effective or which will not be an effective instrument. If we do not get the support of other countries, this Government will advise itself as to the wisest and most effective action to take. In view of the consultations being made, it would be most impolitic to announce beforehand that if members do not hurry up with answers and so forth we would go it alone. It would be most impolitic."

LEGISLATIVE FUNCTION

Most countries are governed by a Constitution, the rule of law and the law making process of Parliament. There are three basic methods of making laws. The first method is where a monarch or a dictator or a small group (an oligarchy or a military junta) can make laws called decrees. This system does not allow the people freedom to approve or reject the laws. They are imposed on the people.

The second method is where all the citizens can come together and vote as was done during the democratic era in ancient Athens. This system is impracticable in a large modern state.[22]

The third method is where the elected representatives of the people exercise their freedom to discuss and scrutinise a proposal called a Bill to make a law.

---

22. *Perhaps the referendum, especially as practised in Switzerland, has taken the place of the Athenian practice.*

The legislative function of Parliament consists in passing Bills and approving statutory instruments where their approval by Parliament is required by law. Clause (2) of article 93 of our Constitution states that,

"Subject to the provisions of this Constitution, the legislative power of Ghana shall be vested in Parliament and shall be exe-cised in accordance with this Constitution"

A person or body other than Parliament does not have the power to make provisions having the force of law except by and under the authority conferred by an Act of Parliament.

Although the Constitution has vested legislative power in Parliament the legislative authority of Parliament is constrained. For example, Parliament cannot pass a law to alter the decision or judgement of any court or pass any law which operates retroactively to adversely affect the personal rights and liberties of a person.[23] Nor can Parliament pass any law to turn Ghana into a one-party state.[24] The Supreme Court can declare any such enactment by Parliament to be unconstitutional.[25]

Bills

The power of Parliament to make laws is exercised by Bills passed by Parliament and assented to by the President.[26]

A Bill may be defined as a draft of a legislative proposal introduced by a Minister or a Private Member which, when passed by the House and assented to by the President becomes a law known as an Act of Parliament.

There are three kinds of Bills – Public, Private and Hybrid. Public Bills deal with matters of general public interest. Private Bills deal with matters of a local or personal interest. Hybrid Bills are at once public and private. Private Bills and Hybrid Bills are not now patronised in our legislature.

Right to introduce Bills

A Bill may be introduced either by a Minister or by a Private Member. In the former case it is called a Government Bill and in the latter case a Private Member's Bill. A Private Member's Bill must not be confused with a Private Bill.

---

23. *Article 107 (b) of the Constitution*
24. *Article 3 of the Constitution*
25. *Article 2 the Constitution*
26. *Article 106 of the Constitution*

Initiation of Bills
A Government Bill takes its rise from a Ministry. A Minister presents a memorandum to the Cabinet proposing that a law should be enacted. The memorandum states the principles and the policy of the proposed legislation, the defects in the existing law and the reason for the introduction of the proposed legislation.

Parliamentary Counsel
An advance copy of the memorandum is sent to Parliamentary Counsel (the lawyers in the Ministry of Justice who draft legislation). When the proposal has been approved, the Ministry concerned is informed by the Cabinet Secretariat, and the head of that Ministry sends drafting instructions to Parliamentary Counsel who proceeds to draft the required legislation. Sometimes the Cabinet itself initiates legislation. In such a case an extract of the minutes of the Cabinet meeting is sent to Parliamentary Counsel and that constitutes drafting instructions. When the draft Bill is approved by the sponsoring Ministry and by the Cabinet it is published in an ordinary issue of the *Gazette* as a Bill at least fourteen days before the date of its introduction in Parliament.

Memorandum accompanying the Bill
In accordance with article 106 of the Constitution a Bill, other than a Bill referred to in article 108 of the Constitution, shall be accompanied by an explanatory memorandum signed by the Minister introducing the Bill in the case of Government Bills, and by the Member introducing the Bill in the case of a Private Member's Bill. The memorandum must set out in detail the policy and principles of the Bill, the defects of the existing law, and the remedies proposed to deal with those defects and the necessity for introducing the Bill. The memorandum is very useful but is not part of the Bill.[27]

Five stages of Bills, certificate of urgency
A Bill must go through five stages: First Reading, Committee Stage, Second Reading, Consideration Stage and Third Reading. All the five stages of a Bill may not be taken at the same Sitting unless a Committee of Parliament certifies that the Bill is of an urgent nature. In that case it may be taken through all its stages at the same Sitting.

---

27. And that is the reason why the Memorandum to the Bill is usually not published as part of the Act. The 1960 Interpretation Act was publihed with the Memorandum to the Bill. The Conveyancing Decree 19 followed that procedure.

Bill affecting Chieftaincy

In accordance with clause (3) of article 106 a Bill affecting the institution of Chieftaincy shall not be introduced in Parliament without prior reference to the National House of Chiefs.

PASSAGE OF BILLS

Presentation and First Reading

When the text of a Bill has been published in the *Gazette*, it may be introduced in the House fourteen days after publication. In the case of Private Member's Bill the leave of the House must be sought before it is introduced. A Bill is presented to the House by the Minister or the Member responsible for that Bill by simply rising in his place and bowing to the Chair upon the Speaker saying: *"Presentation and First Reading of Bills" and calling him by his designation.*

First Reading of a Bill

A motion for the First Reading is not moved. As soon as the Minister or the Private Member bows to the Chair, the Bill is read the first time. A Bill is deemed to have been read when the Clerk reads aloud its long title.[28]

Bill referred to a Committee of the House

When a Bill has been read the first time it is referred to the appropriate Committee of the House which will examine it in detail. The Committee invites the public for its views. It may be noted that this system of referring Bills to appropriate Committees was first introduced by clause (4) of article 106 of the 1969 Constitution which provided for public participation in the legislative process. Bills are closely scrutinised in the Committees.

Second Reading of Bills

Upon the motion, "That this Bill be now read a second time", the Minister or Member introducing the Bill states its principle and general merits. Second Reading is an important stage in the passage of a Bill. The Chairman of the Committee which considered the Bill would then present his report which would form the basis of debate. If the motion is agreed to, the Clerk reads aloud the long title of the Bill and the Bill is then deemed to have been read a second time.

---

28. *It is a reminder of the days when the average Member of Parliament could not read nor write and the Bill in Latin or Norman French was actually read.*

Consideration Stage

When the Bill has been read a second time it goes through the Consideration Stage which is not taken until at least forty-eight hours have elapsed - which period does not include days on which the House does not sit. At the Consideration Stage the Bill is examined in detail clause by clause and amendments proposed to it. The House does not discuss the principle of the Bill at this stage.

Informality of Proceedings

It is only at the Consideration Stage of a Bill that a Member may speak more than once to a question proposed from the Chair. The informality which this concession gives to proceedings at the Consideration Stage is marked by the Marshal tilting the Mace towards the Chair. When the Mace stands upright it indicates formality of the proceedings. The slight change in the angle of the Mace indicates the informal nature of the proceedings at that stage.

At the Consideration Stage of a Bill every part of the Bill must come up for acceptance or rejection. First, the clauses are taken then the schedules and the preamble (if there is one). The last part to be taken is the long title.

Procedure at the Consideration Stage

The procedure is that the Presiding Officer calls the number of each clause in succession and the Clerk reads the marginal note. If an amendment is not proposed, then after a convenient number of clauses has been called the Presiding Officer says, "The question is, That the clauses do ...stand part of the Bill". If while the clauses are being called a Member wishes to move an amendment to a clause or to make some comment on it, the Presiding Officer immediately puts the question on all the clauses which have been called and not yet agreed to excluding the clause the Member wants to be considered.

After each clause has been considered the Presiding Officer says "The question is, That Clauses... stand part of the Bill". When an amendment to the clause has been agreed to, the Presiding Officer says "The question is, That clauses... as amended stand part of the Bill". (When the title of a new clause has been read by the Clerk the clause is deemed to have been read the first time).

The Presiding Officer then says "The question is, That the clause be read a second time", and if the question is agreed to, amendments may at that stage be proposed to the new clause. The final question the

Presiding Officer proposes is. "That the clause (or the clause as amended) be added to the Bill". The Schedules to a Bill and new Schedules proposed are considered and treated in the same way as clauses.

Notices of Amendments

A notice of amendment must bear the heading NOTICE OF AMENDMENT(S) TO BE MOVED AT THE CONSIDERATION OF THE ...BILL. A notice must be signed by the Member proposing the amendment, but in the case of a notice by a Minister it may be signed by an official from his Ministry.

Location and substance of amendment

A notice of amendment consists of two parts: the first part may be called the location of the amendment and the second part the substance of the amendment. The essential constituents of the location are clause or Schedule, page and line. The substance may take the form of (a) deletion, or (b) insertion (or addition) or (c) deletion and insertion (or addition) of other words or figures (instead). The word substitution, which is the same as deletion and insertion (or addition), although found in Acts should not be employed in notices of amendments as it is necessary for the House to consider deletion and insertion (or addition) as two separate questions.

In considering amendments to a clause, the question to be decided by the House relates to the whole clause. Therefore, although the amendment is in fact going to affect only a subclause or a paragraph of that clause, only the clause itself should be stated in the notice.

Use of insert and add

Where a clause is being augmented, *insert* is used unless the augmenting words are to be put at the end of the clause, in which case *add* is used. Phrases like "the word" and "the figure", although found in Acts of Parliament, should not be employed in a notice of amendment. All that is necessary is to put quotation marks immediately before and after the words or figures. If punctuation marks or signs form part of an amendment, they are embraced by the quotation marks.

Reference to lines

Where words are to be inserted in a new line, the line immediately after which the words are to be inserted should be stated in the notice, in which case the phrase "thereafter insert" should be used. Where the words to be deleted occur in more than one line, only the first line should be stated in the notice. Where a whole subclause or paragraph is to be deleted, only the first line of that subclause or paragraph should be stated in the notice.

Deletion of a whole clause
An amendment to delete a whole clause is not usually admissible. The correct procedure is to put this down as an amendment to delete the clause and underline the whole of the amendment which should be embraced by brackets. It will then be printed in the Notice Paper in italics within brackets. Upon the clause being called the Member proposing the amendment should invite the House to vote against it. If it is rejected the Presiding Officer says, "Clause ...disagreed to". The phrase disagreed to is used only in this circumstance.

The marginal note to a clause does not form part of the Bill, and if deletion or insertion becomes necessary consequent on an amendment to the clause, the required action is taken by the Clerk.

Adjustments by Clerk
The numbering of new clauses and subclauses and the numbering or lettering of new paragraphs as well as the renumbering of clauses and subclauses necessitated by an amendment are undertaken by the Clerk. The renumbering or relettering should not be proposed as an amendment, nor should numbers or letters be anticipated for new clauses, subclauses and paragraphs.

Deletion and insertion of punctuation marks consequential on an amendment are also undertaken by the Clerk. The deletion or insertion should not be proposed as an amendment. An example is the substitution of a full stop or semi-colon for the colon at the end of the line immediately preceding a proviso upon that proviso being deleted. Printing errors which are trivial should not be proposed as amendments.

They should be merely brought to the notice of the Clerk. The following examples of amendments are given as a guide:

(i)   Clause 4, page 3, line 47, delete "¢50,000.00" and insert ¢30,000.00".

(ii) Clause 5, page 4, line 24, delete "against loss resulting from failure".

(iii) Clause 8, page 6, line 43, delete from "As" to "fifty-five" in line 2, page 7.

(iv) Clause 10,page 8, line 7, delete subclause (2).

(v) Clause 12, page 10, line 18, delete paragraph (k) and insert the following new paragraph: "The Minster shall conserve the areas for industrial operations". (Note that new paragraph bears no letter).

(vi) Clause 14, page 11, line 10, thereafter, insert "Where it appears to the Officer ...he may immediately order the seizure of the goods" (Note that new subclause bears no number).

(vii) Clause 16, page 17, at end, add "and the Regulations shall be deemed to have been complied with". (Note the use of add as distinct from insert. The word add shows that the amendment is at the end of the clause and it is therefore unnecessary to state the line).

(viii) Clause 18, page 9, lines 2,3, 7 and 11 delete "Minister of Finance" and insert "Accountant-General".

(ix) Clause 20, page 7, line 5, delete the quotation marks before and after "district".

(x) Clause 16, page 12, line 15, delete from "Commissioner" first occurring to "area" second occurring in line 17.

(xi) Third Schedule, page 14, line 32, Tenth Column, after "69" insert 71".

(xii) [Delete Clause 26]

(Note that Clause 26 being in italics and within brackets is meant to be rejected).

Third Reading

After a Bill has passed through the Consideration Stage its final stage may be taken. The motion "That this Bill be now read the third time" is a formal one and does not lead to debate.

Rejection of Bills

At the Second or Third Reading of a Bill an amendment may be proposed to reject the Bill. Upon the motion, "That this Bill be now read a second (or the third) time" being moved, a Member may move to delete the words "be read a second (or the third) time" and to insert the words "be rejected". If that amendment is agreed to, the Bill has been rejected.

Reasoned amendment

A Member may alternatively move a reasoned amendment by deleting all the words after the word "That" and adding words stating the object and motive on which his opposition to the Bill is based.

Withdrawal and lapsing of Bill

A Member who has introduced a Bill may withdraw it upon motion made at any stage.

All the stages of a Bill need not be taken at the same meeting. Formerly if at the end of a Session a Bill had not been passed it automatically lapsed through the effect of prorogation. (Now under clause (1) of article 113 of the Constitution, Parliament continues for a period of four years from the date of its first sitting and then stands dissolved. There is no prorogation. Bills do not therefore lapse at the end of the Session.)

Passing of Bills

A Bill is not passed by the House unless it has passed through all the five stages that is, the First Reading, Committee Stage, a Second Reading, the Consideration Stage and the Third Reading.

Assent to Bills

When a Bill has been passed the text as passed is printed on vellum. On each of the four printed copies the Clerk certifies that the printed impression is a true copy of the Bill which the House has passed. The Bill is then presented to the President after the Presidential Seal has been affixed to the copies. The President signifies his assent to the Bill by signing it under the words "I hereby signify my assent to this Bill". If the President does not like some of the provisions of the Bill, he may refuse to assent to these provisions. If he refuses to assent to the whole of a Bill, he does not sign it. This does not prejudice the right of a Member to introduce the Bill again.

In accordance with clause (7) of article 106 of the Constitution, Standing Order No. 134, the President should signify his assent or refusal within seven days to the Speaker after a Bill has been passed by Parliament and presented to him. If he refuses to assent to a Bill he should within fourteen days of the refusal state in a memorandum to the Speaker any specific provisions of the Bill which he thinks should be reconsidered by Parliament including his recommendations for amendments.

The President could also under paragraph (b) of clause (8) of article 106, inform the Speaker that he has referred the Bill to the Council of State for consideration and comment under article 90 of the Constitution.

When the Bill has been reconsidered by Parliament and passed by a resolution supported by the votes of not less than two-thirds of all Members, the President shall give assent to the Bill within thirty days of the passing of the resolution.[29]

Commencement of Acts

Article 106 (11) of the Constitution provides that without prejudice to the power of Parliament to postpone the operation of a law, a Bill shall not become law until it has been duly passed and assented to in accordance with the Constitution and shall not come into force unless it has been published in the Gazette.

Reflections on the Legislative Process

Our legislative process is deliberately slow. The slow method may even be said to be caution in excess. That weakness is Parliament's strength. Against the backdrop of our past experience in the First Republic when many Bills including the infamous Preventive Detention Bill were passed upon Certificate of Urgency, the framers of our Constitutions since 1969 felt that because we are governed by the rule of law it is essential that each piece of legislation introduced in Parliament is given adequate time for effective scrutiny. The laws Parliament makes affect every citizen. Therefore before a Bill becomes an Act, public participation in the process is essential.

The process requires that a Bill (apart from a Bill of an urgent nature which a Committee of Parliament has so certified) must be published in the Gazette fourteen days before its introduction in Parliament. The Gazette notification gives the public an opportunity to study the Bill. After the Bill has been introduced it is not immediately dealt with but is referred to a Committee of the House for detailed examination and report to the House.

At the Committee level the electorate and the elected Members can meet to consider the Bill. Public input into the legislative process is essential. It has helped to improve the quality of legislation. The various stages of Bills are meant to ensure that the legislature hastens slow-

---

29. *Article 106 (10) of the Constitution*

ly in order to avoid hasty and improper adoption of laws, especially as we do not have a Second Chamber which could act as a revising chamber.

Approval of delegated legislation
The legislative function is also exercised by the examination and approval of statutory instruments, that is Orders, Rules, Regulations or Bye-laws made by bodies other than Parliament under powers delegated to them by Acts of Parliament. An enabling Act, that is the Act delegating the power, sometimes declares that an instrument made under it is to be subject to annulment by Parliament. The instrument is required to be laid before Parliament and is to be published in the Gazette on the day it is laid before Parliament. The instrument is deemed to be revoked if within twenty-one days Parliament resolves by two-thirds of all Members of Parliament that it should be annuled. On the other hand the instrument automatically comes into force if a resolution is not passed by Parliament at the expiration of twenty-one days.

By clause (7) of article 11 of the Constitution, any Orders, Rules or Regulations should be laid before Parliament, should be published in the Gazette, and "come into force at the expiration of twenty-one sitting days after being so laid unless Parliament, before the expiration of the twenty-one days annuls the Order, Rules or Regulation by the votes of not less than two-thirds of all the Members of Parliament"

FINANCIAL FUNCTION

Budget Statement
The financial function of Parliament is carried out by (a) consideration of the proposed use of public funds as set out in the Estimates submitted by the Government and (b) consideration of proposals for the imposition of taxes by which the Government intends to raise money to meet its proposed expenditure. Shortly after the Sessional Address, the Minister of Finance makes his Budget Statement. Before then the President is required by the Constitution to cause to be prepared and laid before Parliament at least one month before the end of the financial year, estimates of the revenues and expenditures of the Government.[30] In his Budget Statement the Minister of Finance reviews the state of the national economy and informs Parliament of his tax proposals for the new Session.

---

30. Article 179 (1) of the Constitution

Provisional, Annual and Supplementary Estimates and vote on account

Estimates are of three kinds: Provisional, Annual and Supplementary. Estimates are also divided into parts, the Consolidated Fund and the Development Fund being treated together in the same part. The money voted upon Provisional Estimates immediately after the Budget Statement is known as a Vote on Account. The purpose of the Vote on Account in accordance with article 180 of the Constitution is to enable the various public services to meet expenditure until the expenditure Warrants are signed upon the approval of the Annual Estimates. If the Government wants more money after the Annual Estimates have been approved, it submits Supplementary Estimates. The Government may require more money (a) if the money granted in respect of any Head of the Annual Estimates proves to be insufficient, or (b) because expenditure is required in respect of a Head not included in those Estimates.

Virement

It should be noted that Parliament only deals with Heads of Estimates. When it approves an amount to be spent under a particular Head, the whole or a part of that amount may not be transferred to another Head without its authority. A transfer from one Subhead to another under the same Head is effected by a power known as *virement* which is exercised by the Minister of Finance. A vote of Parliament approving a Head of Estimate is sufficient authority for the amount under that Head to be spent. Parliament has ceased to entrench the moneys it votes in an Appropriation Act.

Supply days

The Business Committee allots a number of days for the consideration of the Annual Budget. On the last allotted day all Heads which have not been considered are brought up for approval en bloc. The ostensible purpose of the laborious exercise of considering the Annual Estimates is to enable Members to probe the minutiae of proposed public expenditure. The real purpose, however, is to cause Ministers to declare and defend the policies of the departments under them. Parliament has the right to reduce the budget as it sees fit but cannot increase it.

Appropriation Bill

When Parliament has concluded its consideration of the Annual Estimates, an Appropriation Bill is introduced to grant the amount of money Parliament has agreed to supply. The Government does not have the authority to spend public money until the Appropriation Bill is passed. However, the Constitution provides in article 180 that where it appears to the President that the Appropriation Act in respect of a financial year will not come into operation at the beginning of that financial year, he may with the prior approval of Parliament, authorise temporary financing for three months.

Contingencies Fund
As it is not practicable to summon Parliament to approve expenditure of sums which have not been voted by it and which are required urgently, a Contingencies Fund has been established under article 177 of the Constitution. The Committee on Finance may authorise advances to be made from that Fund to meet urgent or unforeseen need for expenditure for which no other provision exists to meet that need. A supplementary estimate is presented to Parliament as soon as possible to replace the amount so advanced.

How Parliament Exercises Its Financial Control
To be able to exercise control over government expenditure, Parliament must be given financial information on how government raises and spends money. Government must therefore inform Parliament before it can give approval to its proposals. A great deal of information is provided in the Annual Estimates - how much money government needs and how it will be spent. Article 179(1) of the Constitution compels the government to provide the Estimates one month before the end of the Financial Year, which are closely scrutinized by the House through its Committees and the House as a whole after presentation of the Budget Statement by the Minister of Finance.

a. Supply Days
In order to ensure effective control over financial matters, Parliament has a supply procedure in which each estimate is examined over a fixed number of days that are allotted to Committees. As we have explained earlier, the purpose of the laborious exercise of considering the Annual Estimates is not only to enable Members to probe the minutiae of the proposed public expenditure, but also to cause Ministers to declare and defend the policies of the departments under them.

It has been said that 'supply alone affords members that right of criticism, that constant power of demanding from the government explanations of their administrative and executive action, without which supply can never be possessed'.[31] Supply days give the Minority groups opportunities to criticize government policy and administration on subjects of public interest.

After the consideration of the Estimates the House has power to accept or reduce them. The government must obtain legislative approval for the expenditure in the form of an Appropriation Bill. The money so approved must be appropriated for the purposes for which they were originally requested by government.

b. Power to impose, vary or waive taxes

Article 174(2) of the Constitution empowers Parliament to impose, vary or waive taxes. Standing Order 169 gives power to the Finance Committee to examine tax waiver and make appropriate recommendation to Parliament.

Members have the opportunity of registering objection to specific taxation proposals in the budget. Even though they may not be able to throw out the proposals, their right to criticize and seek explanation from the Executive ensures that the incidence of taxes are less oppressive.

By approving the Estimates and the Appropriation Act, Parliament exercises its ultimate authority over government expenditure. Parliament can accept or reject the budget; it can refuse Minister's supply or reduce it if it is dissatisfied with the performance of any government department. These controls at least, ensure that government must respect the will of the democratically elected Parliament.

c. Parliamentary approval for loans

A loan the Government wants to raise on behalf of itself or any other public institution must be authorized by Parliament by virtue of article 181 of the Constitution. The Finance Committee of the House also plays a much more positive role in monitoring foreign exchange receipts and payments or transfers.

d. Watchdog role of Public Accounts Committees

After the passage of the Appropriation Bill, the financial watchdog role of Parliament is exercised through its Public Accounts Committee.

---

31. Arthur Balfour, First Secretary of the Treasury in Parliamentary Debates (1896), 37 Ch. 724-6
Parliament and Congress pp. 314-315
Kenneth Bradshaw and David Pring.

At the end of the fiscal year when the money has been spent, the public expenditure is thoroughly audited by the Auditor-General whose report is examined by the Public Accounts Committee. The Chairman of the Committee is either the Minority Leader or the Minority spokesperson on Finance. The audited account will show how much money has actually been spent for each vote for which money was granted in the Appropriation Act.

The Committee determines whether all expenditures were incurred with proper legislative authority. The committee also examines whether there has been waste or extravagance or misapplication or overspending or under-spending. The watchdog role of the Minority side over Government spending is one of the important oversight functions of Parliament.

e. Financial role of Parliament is limited

In practical terms, the financial role of Parliament is limited. First, it is only the Government or the Executive that can take financial initiative, which means that Parliament itself does not appropriate money unless the Executive requires such taxation.

The Constitution has vested the power of initiating expenditure in the Government while Parliament confines itself with the role of approving, supplying, appropriating and criticizing how government spends moneys granted to it. Parliament can only reduce expenditure if it is dissatisfied with the performance of government departments.

The limitation of the Parliamentary financial role is constitutional and cannot be changed without amending the relevant provisions of Chapter Thirteen of the Constitution.

Chapter Five

POWERS, PRIVILEGES AND IMMUNITIES OF PARLIAMENT [32]

Essential nature of Parliamentary privileges and immunities
Parliamentary privileges and immunities are special rights enjoyed by the Speaker, Members of Parliament and Officers of Parliament. These rights are intended to protect their actions in the course of performing their parliamentary functions. Without this protection, which is not available to other citizens, Members would be severely restricted in the performance of their functions. They would be vulnerable to pressures and temptations from powerful Governments and pressure groups who would seek to muzzle them by taking legal action against them or intimidating them in the course of their duties. The authority of the House to scrutinize the actions of the Executive and the use of the House as a forum for ventilating grievances of the electorate would also be severely constrained. Parliamentary privileges and immunities are therefore essential to the status and authority of Parliament.

Main Privileges

The main privileges as provided in the Constitution are:
Freedom of speech, debate and proceedings in Parliament. That freedom cannot be impeached or questioned in any court or place out of Parliament in accordance with Article 115 of the Constitution. One of the strengths of parliamentary democracy is that matters of national importance must be fully and openly discussed in the House without fear or favour. This privilege applies only to speeches made in the House or its precincts. It does not confer a licence on Members to say whatever they like.

Unsubstantiated allegations not permitted
Unsubstantiated allegations are not generally permitted. However, the freedom to make allegations which a Member in good faith believes to

---

32. *The substance of this Chapter is based on a Paper delivered by the author at the Commonwealth Parliamentary Association Africa Regional Conference in Accra in 1997.*

be true or at least worthy of investigation is regarded as fundamental. It has been said that there will be no freedom of speech if everything said has to be proved true before it was uttered. An interesting case of privilege involving an MP may be cited. On the 12th of August, 1958 Hon. B. K. Adama, a prominent Opposition Member, made a speech in the House in which he referred to a document in his possession as "Secret Cabinet Paper", during a debate on a Motion made by the Government side. The House resolved that Adama's pronouncement on that document should be referred to the Committee of Privileges for it to determine whether the document was genuine or fabricated and in the light of its findings to report whether the MP had committed a breach of privilege.

It was forcefully argued that at the time the Member made the speech he believed the genuineness of the document. A Committee Member said that if the majority side had read the document they would have concluded it was genuine. Asked what action he as a good politician took in relation to his Party, Adama answered that he thought the most appropriate action was to bring the document to the notice of Parliament by mentioning it in Parliament as he did not want to make political capital out of it. He could have mentioned it on a political platform to his advantage during the campaign for local government elections.

The burning question was: Did Adama at the material time knowingly utter a false document in the House? Although the House found him guilty of contempt his apology was accepted amid shouts of "Hear, hear". The allegation was worthy of investigation. At least it helped to kill rumours.

Immunity from service of process and arrest
A civil or criminal process issuing from any court or place out of Parliament may not be served on, or executed in relation to, the Speaker or a Member while he is on his way to, attending, or returning from a proceeding of Parliament, except with the Speaker's permission in the case of a criminal process. A civil or criminal proceeding may not be instituted against a Member in a court or place out of Parliament for anything he has said in Parliament or any matter he has brought before it. The Speaker, Members and Officers of Parliament enjoy immunity from service as jurors or assessors and from giving evidence in court during meetings of Parliament.[33]

---

33. *Articles 115 to 121 of the Constitution are helpful in these matters*

CONTEMPT OF PARLIAMENT [34]

Contempt defined
An act which impedes or tends to impede the House in the performance of its functions or affronts its dignity may constitute contempt of Parliament or a breach of parliamentary privilege.

The main types of contempt are:
   (a) *assaulting or insulting the Speaker or a Member while he is within the precincts of the House or on his way to, attending or returning from any of its proceedings;*[35]
   (b) *creating a disturbance which interrupts the proceedings of the House or a Committee;*
   (c) *giving false evidence to the House or a Committee with intent to deceiving it;*
   (d) *publishing a matter which falsely or scandalously defames the House or the Speaker, a Member or an Officer in his official capacity;*
   (e) *misconduct by Members or officers in the nature of deliberately misleading the House; and corruption by acceptance of bribes;*
   (f) *endeavouring by means of bribery, fraud or the infliction, or threatened infliction, of violence, restraint or spiritual or temporary injury to influence a Member in the performance of his functions;*
   (g) *disobedience to rules or orders of the House or a Committee, in the nature of refusal to attend as a witness and refusing an order to withdraw from the House.*

Punishment of offenders
The House has the power to protect its privilege and to impose sanctions against its breach. It is well established that without the power to punish offenders laws would become meaningless. Although the Constitution and the Standing Orders of the House are silent on the kind of punishment for those found guilty of contempt or breach of privilege, the following punishments may be imposed:

---

34. *See articles 122 and 123 of the Constitution*
35. *A particular case may be cited: In 1965 a female activist of the ruling Party assaulted Miss Regina Asamany, a Deputy Minister, in the precincts of the House. This happened in the presence of the author after the adjournment of the House. The matter was investigated by the Committee of Privileges which reported that there was a fracas, so the matter was rested.*

*(a) A Member found by the House to be guilty of contempt
        may be reprimanded in his place in the House by the
        Speaker or be suspended from the service of the House for
        a specific period or expelled from the House;*

*(b) Expulsion as the ultimate punishment for a Member demonstrates
        the power of the House to regulate its own proceedings.*

Punishment of Officers, of strangers

An Officer found guilty of contempt may be suspended from duty in
Parliament and may have disciplinary proceedings taken against him by the
Parliamentary Service Board. A stranger found guilty of contempt may be
excluded from the precincts of the House or reprimanded by the Speaker at
the Bar of the House or have criminal proceedings taken against him in a
court. Under article 123 of the Constitution, "the exercise by Parliament of
the power to punish for contempt shall not be a bar to the institution of proceedings under the Criminal Law". Parliament itself cannot impose a fine
or a prison sentence.

Procedure for Raising Complaints of Privilege by Members

A Member who wishes to raise a matter of contempt in the House
should first submit a written notice to the Speaker as soon as possible
after the alleged breach of privilege has occurred. The notice may
include supporting documents or evidence. The Speaker would then
consider the matter and give or withhold his consent to further proceedings. When the matter is of an urgent nature and there is no time to
give notice, the Speaker may permit a Member to raise the matter in the
House, by making a short statement relevant to the question of privilege. The matter may be decided by the House or referred by it to the
Committee of Privileges for examination and report to the House. The
Motion is usually debated and there is often a division of opinion especially where the matter has a political flavour. If an apology is received
from the offender the Motion may either be withdrawn or not moved at
all.

Restraint in enforcing privileges

The Speaker, Members and Officers of Parliament enjoy the special
privileges which are not available to the citizens they represent. This
sets the House apart from the people but not in a discriminatory sense.
While there is the need to maintain these privileges the House itself
should exercise restraint and not always seek to enforce these privileges
except when it is satisfied that not to do so will jeopardise its dignity.

Chapter six

COMMITTEES OF PARLIAMENT
Committees of Parliament perform the very real and important task of
Parliament for which all the two hundred Members cannot effectively
carry out in the Chamber. Committees are required, for example, to
examine in detail Bills that are introduced into Parliament. They are to
make inquiries and investigate matters that are complex and complicat-
ed outside the Chamber. Committees of different kinds and for different tasks can undertake these complex tasks.

Committee of Selection and Standing Committees
At the first meeting of a new Parliament a Committee of Selection
under the chairmanship of the Speaker is appointed to prepare lists of
chairpersons, vicechairpersons and Members to compose the Standing
Committees:
- (a) the Standing Orders Committee;
- (b) the Business Committee;
- (c) the Committee of Privileges;
- (d) the Public Accounts Committee;
- (e) the House Committee;
- (f) the Finance Committee;
- (g) the Appointments Committee
- (h) the Committee on Members Holding Office of profit; and
- (i) the Committee on Government Assurances

Every Member of Parliament in accordance with clause (4) of article
103 of the Constitution, should serve on at least one of the Standing
Committees.

Standing Committees are permanent and the tradition is that once
appointed under clause (2) of article 103 of the Constitution they cannot be disbanded. The size of the Committees ranges from fifteen to
thirty-one and Members are chosen by their parties in proportion to
their numerical strength in the House.

Oversight function of Committees
Parliament is not only concerned with making laws. It is also concerned
with holding the Government to account in respect of its policies and
administration. One of the important devices for enabling the House to

exercise effective check on the Government is the establishment of the specialist Committees.

Backbenchers from both sides of the House can exercise vigilance on Government activities especially if they operate in a non-partisan environment in Committees.

Select Committees
The following Select Committees have been established:

(a) the Committee on Food, Agriculture and Cocoa Affairs;

(b) the Committee on Lands and Forestry;

(c) the Committee on Health;

(d) the Committee on Constitutional, Legal and Parliamentary Affairs;

(e) the Committee on Works and Housing;

(f) the Committee on Local Government and Rural Development;

(g) the Committee on Foreign Affairs;

(h) the Committee on Employment, Social Welfare and State Enterprises;

(i) the Committee on Communications;

(j) the Committee on Defence and the Interior;

(k) the Committee on Trade, Industry and Tourism;

(l) the Committee on Environment, Science and Technology;

(m) the Committee on Education

(n) the Committee on Youth, Sports and Culture;

(o) the Committee on Mines and Energy; and

(p) the Committee on Roads and Transport.

Ad hoc Committees may be appointed to deal with an unexpected matter that requires investigation and decision.

Powers of the Committees
The Committees enjoy the powers, rights and privileges that are vested in the High Court of Justice or a Justice of the High Court at a trial, in respect of:

(a) enforcing the attendance of witnesses and examining them on oath, affirmation or otherwise;

(b) compelling the production of documents; and

(c) the issue of a commission or request to examine witnesses abroad.

Duties of Standing Committees

The Committee of Privileges enquires into complaints of contempt of Parliament and matters of privilege which may be referred to it.

The House Committee considers and advises the Speaker upon matters connected with the comfort and convenience of Members.

The Public Accounts Committee examines the accounts showing the appropriation of the sums granted by Parliament to meet public expenditure and any other accounts laid before Parliament that are referred to it, together with the Auditor-General's report on the accounts. It also advises on changes that may be considered desirable in the form of the Estimates. The Committee also examines the accounts of a statutory body which have been laid before Parliament. The Committee has the power to travel to and meet in places that it considers necessary.

The Public Accounts Committee must report to Parliament at least twice in a year. The Minority Leader or Opposition "Spokesman" on Finance is usually chairman of the Committee.

The Business Committee determines the business of each Sitting and the order in which it is to be taken. The Majority Leader is the chairman of the Committee and the Minority Leader is a member of the Committee.

The Standing Orders Committee considers and reports to Parliament proposals for the amendment of the Standing Orders.

AN OVERVIEW OF THE COMMITTEE SYSTEM IN PARLIAMENT OF GHANA[36]

Committees of the First Republic

The Parliaments of Ghana from 1957 to 1966 did not develop a committee system that could offer effective solutions to some of the weaknesses in the democratic process.

The committees of these parliaments were classified into Sessional Select Committees and Ad hoc Committees. There were five Select Committees: the House Committee, the Business Committee, the Committee of Privileges, the Public Accounts Committee and the Standing Orders Committee whose traditional functions are well-known. These Committees could only make recommendations for adoption by the House, but when so empowered by the House, they

---

36. *The substance of this topic is based on a paper delivered by the author at a workshop on capacity building for the leadership in Parliament organized by the Ghana Centre for Democratic Development - CDD at Akosombo in February 2003.*

could take a decision. The Sessional Select Committees were appointed at the beginning of each session for the duration of that session. The Party Whips nominated membership to the committees. Ad Hoc Committees were appointed as and when the need arose.

The absence of a virile committee system prevented Parliament from exercising its effective scrutiny function of holding the Government to account in respect of its policies and administration and to ensure effective parliamentary and public scrutiny of legislative proposals called Bills and loan agreements.

It may, however, be noted that Parliament faced several constraints. Among other things, it lacked space and committee rooms; it had a Reading Room that was called a Library, but without Research Assistants. There was a shortage of qualified staff to service committees. In fact there were only four Clerks: The Clerk to Parliament and his Deputy and two Assistant Clerks. Funding and government support to provide effective committee system was not a priority.

The only active Committee was the Public Accounts Committee which produced outstanding reports. It was the only committee that some Ministers and Public Servants dreaded and were reluctant to appear before. It was felt that, in that prevailing atmosphere, committees that delved deep into issues and whose reports were critical were not overly welcomed by the government.

Committee System Introduced in Second Republic
The 1969 Constitution of the Second Republic, the 1979 and 1992 Constitutions of the Third and Fourth Republics respectively, made provisions for the Committee System. The three constitutions recognized that in the past many Bills were passed upon Certificate of Urgency presented to the House by the President and too many decisions were taken without public consultation.

The Constitution makers recognized that the public, for whom Parliament exists, must understand how the institution makes laws that affect them and what avenues are open to them to be involved in the legislative process. The three constitutions reinforced the importance of committees as an ideal vehicle for public participation in the legislative process and public policy formulation. The Chamber of Parliament does not provide a forum for public participation in debates. The Committees offer less formal and less intimidating atmosphere for public participation in policy-making and the legislative process.

An essential provision in the Constitution is that every legislative proposal (a bill), after its first reading, must be referred to a committee that invites public participation in the legislative process. The Committee to which a bill has been referred must report to the House before the second reading and other stages of the bill can be taken.

It is at the committee level that both the elected and the electorates can meet to discuss policies and legislative proposals. Such a meeting has an educational value for Parliament and the public. They learn from each other. An interaction of this nature is helpful to disabuse the minds of the electorate that MPs are aloof and divorced from the people they represent.

Types of Committees

Article 103(4) of the Constitution also requires that every Member must belong to at least one of the Standing Committees. It has been observed that if a Member belongs to more than two Committees, he spreads himself too thin to be effective.

The Constitution has provided for the establishment of Standing Committees to which every member including Ministers must belong. In addition, Select Committees exist by virtue of the Standing Orders and Committee members are selected from backbenchers. And from time to time Ad Hoc Committees are set up to consider a particular problem on a matter of public importance.

Powers of Committees in Parliament

The functions and powers of our committees are circumscribed by the rules laid down in the Standing Orders of the House. Parliament is reluctant to allow committees much scope or initiative to make inquiry into matters that have not been referred to them by the House. The Committees have had to operate in the shadow of the House that created them. This may be understandable because, unlike the Congress, our Parliament is not omnipotent in law making. For example, our Parliament cannot pass legislation to make Ghana a one party state. Since Parliament is not all-powerful in law making, it logically follows that its committees cannot operate beyond the powers granted them by the superior body (i.e. Parliament).

Although constrained, the Committees are sufficiently well armed to carry out the tasks given them. The Committees can compel the production of documents and papers relevant to their inquiry. They can also require the attendance of witnesses and examine them on oath or affirmation. They can send for anyone who can assist them in their inquiry. Refusal to attend to the Committees may be treated as contempt and punished accordingly.

However, by convention, the power to send for persons does not include the right to issue summons to Members to attend and give evidence. They may be invited to do so.

A Committee can also choose any topic it likes within its broad terms of reference and organize site visits to hear evidence and study operations of projects at close quarters.

Appointment of Chairpersons and Vice-Chairpersons

The Standing Orders have given powers to the Committee of Selection whose Chairperson is the Speaker, to appoint the Chairperson and Vice-Chairperson of most Committees. The chairs of some Committees such as the Committee of Privileges, Standing Orders Committee and Appointments Committee have been designated by the Standing Orders of the House.

Chairpersons of committees are not evenly spread among the Parties. Most chairpersons are pre-selected and appointed from the Majority Party. But Committees such as the Public Accounts and the Committee on Statutory Instruments have their chairpersons selected from the Minority Party. But these committees, like all other committees, have the majority of their members selected from the Majority Party to reflect party strengths in the House in accordance with Article 103(5) of the Constitution.

The Role of Committee Chairpersons

It may be helpful to draw a comparison between the role of the congressional committee chairman and parliamentary committee chairman. The former exercises a great deal of power and influence. The Chair in the Congressional Committee system is appointed by seniority from the majority party. He can determine his committee's agenda and (sometimes decide when the committee should meet). He can decide which of the many bills referred to the committee should be considered and in what order. By this arrangement, he can expedite, retard and even stifle bills at his convenience. He can decide which witnesses shall be heard by the committee and he leads the questioning. He has the power to punish breaches of order and decorum at committee meetings.

The Chairperson plays a dominant role in the recruitment and organization of committee staff and controls the expenditure of the committee. He supervises the writing of the committee's report to the House or he nominates a member to do so. He has the power to create sub-committees and to nominate their members to whom he can refer bills. The sub-committee may have their own staff and sizeable budget of their own. The extent of power and influence of a congressional committee chairman is enormous. It is therefore not surprising that Woodrow Wilson described the American system of government as "a government by the Chairmen of the Standing Committees of Congress".[37]

In contrast, the role of the Chairman of the parliamentary committee is constrained. He is appointed by the leadership of his party and not by the committee itself on seniority. He presides over the meetings of the committee by applying standing orders or procedure set by resolution to ensure procedural fairness. When he takes the chair, it is the members of the committee who decide on the agenda, the witnesses to be heard and how the inquiry is to be conducted.

At each meeting the Chairman leads the questioning of each witness. But other members who may wish to raise other points may interrupt him. He can close a meeting to the public in accordance with Standing Order 199 and can remove disruptive persons from the committee room in an open sitting. At the conclusion of an inquiry, he directs the Clerk to produce a draft of the report with the assistance of specialist advisers (in the case of Public Accounts Committee, the Auditor-General and Controller and Accountant-General). The draft is put before the Committee for its consideration. Amendment may be proposed by other Members and vote taken on it. He and the Clerk sign the report of the Committee for presentation to the House and he moves a motion for its adoption by the House.

In our parliamentary committee system, a committee (not the Chair alone) can set up a sub-committee only on the authority of the House depending on workload. When the committee is given power it decides who the members and chairman of a sub-committee should be. A sub-committee will report to the parent committee which issues the report as its own.

While the congressional committee can employ its own staff (professional and clerical staff), the parliamentary committees have their staff assigned to them from the Clerk's department by the Clerk of the House who is the accounting officer.

The Congressional Committee Staff are employees of the Committee while those in parliamentary committees and sub-committees are employees of the House. The work done by the support staff in

---

37. *Parliament and Congress p. 238–239*
   Kenneth Bradshaw and David Pring

both congressional and parliamentary committees include advising the chairman and members, writing reports and handling administrative problems.

The Chairperson of a parliamentary Committee is the committee's spokesperson with the Presiding Officer (i.e. Speaker) in the House and in correspondence with Ministers and senior government officials. He consults the leadership of the House, particularly the Chairman of the Business Committee with regard to presentation of the committee's report to the House and date for debate on it.

Constraints on Parliamentary Committees

We are inclined to believe that our hybrid system of government is designed to ensure that the Executive and Parliament are working along the same lines. Through constraints on both Committees and Parliament the system does not encourage rivalry between Parliament and the Executive.

Some of the factors that constrain Parliament and its Committees in their oversight of the Executive are:

- The bulk of the legislation is initiated by the Executive. It is a daunting task for private members to initiate bills in Parliament. The Private Member needs funding, drafting assistance and support from the government.
- Parliament does not vote (appropriate) money unless the Executive proposes it, nor does the House impose or increase taxes unless the Executive requires such taxation.
- The bulk of the time in the House is taken up in government business.

Although constrained by limited resources and time, the committees can exercise effective scrutiny of government on particular subjects that the government would prefer the Committees to leave alone. The Public Accounts Committee, for example, can interrogate Ministers and Senior Civil Servants in a way that the House itself cannot do through the use of Question Time. Committee's pressure can contribute to a change in government policy.

Committee Capacity Building

The House and its Committees can choose to defeat a government bill or motion and influence government policy. But the Committees can-not expect to do a thorough job of matters referred to them unless we strengthen their capacity. Several of the constraints faced by Parliaments of the three republics are still with us. Lack of space, funding and well trained support staff are some of the problems that must be given priority attention. An effective Committee structure must be well equipped with facilities and services for its operations. Efficient support staff and funds to hire persons with expertise outside the House must be available to the Committees. Because legislative business has grown in volume and become complex the Chairpersons and Members need a certain amount of specialized knowledge to carry out their functions. They must have the tools to do their work which include information services, that is a well equipped Parliamentary Library with research and reference facilities. Without access to well processed information, members cannot make well-informed contributions to debate. Uninformed debates are not helpful but ill-informed contributions to debated on complex issues are more dangerous.

To avoid this, the Chairpersons and Members need to upgrade their skills through seminars and workshops, and study visits to other Parliaments. Ideally, the Chairpersons and Members must be provided with office accommodation.

Conclusion

Looking back, it is heartening to observe that the committee system has made steady progress since its introduction from the Second Republic to the Fourth Republic. The confrontational style of politics and the rigid preconceived positions held by both sides of the House during the First Republic have given way to less adversarial politics and consensus building on matters of national interest at the committee level.

However, when it comes to party discipline, Members still have limited scope of independent action at the committee level. Individual members must express their views freely. Indeed, dispassionate approach to issues in order to reach the truth will enhance public confidence in its committee system. In this regard, the Public Accounts Committee must be commended for its non-partisan approach to its work.

Chapter Seven

RECORDS OF PARLIAMENT - A Miscellany

Minutes

The official record of proceedings in Parliament is called Minutes. These are essentially a record of *res gestae*,[38] for example, the Three Readings of a Bill and the decisions taken on motions.

Official Report

The complete record of proceedings is called the Official Report, commonly known as Hansard. Proceedings in the House are taken down by shorthand and the Official Report is as near as possible verbatim. A Member may suggest corrections to the transcript of his speech before the Official Report is printed, but the corrections must be confined to grammar and spelling.

The Official Report should not be confused with the Official Record. The latter is prepared by the Clerk and the former produced by officials of Parliament, under the supervision of the Editor of Debates.

Correction of the Minutes and the Official Record

Points of order concerning the accuracy of the Minutes – (Votes and Proceedings) or the Official Report may be raised at the time appointed for Personal Statements.

Hansard

One of the important functions of Members of Parliament is to inform the electorate about the activities of Government. Members themselves must be well informed to be able to carry out this duty.

The provision of relevant information is therefore essential for effective and efficient functioning of Parliament. Without access to reliable information, Members cannot expect to be well informed about proposals brought before the House for effective scrutiny.

A reliable working paper is a necessary tool Members need to do their work. The business of the House, except in urgent circumstance, requires adequate notice before it is considered. This means that notice previously given for every business item must be printed or published

---

38. *Things done or matters of fact.*

and made available for Members. Debates and decisions of the House are required to be accurately and speedily recorded and made available for Members to enable them to effectively participate in the proceedings of the House. Hansard is one of the important and reliable official documents that is daily available for the work in Parliament.

Hansard, its origin

Proceedings in Parliament are taken down by shorthand. They are as nearly as possible verbatim and they are printed as the "Official Report", that is the report produced by officials of Parliament under the supervision of the Editor of Debates. The "Official Report" is commonly known as **Hansard**, the name of a private printer and publisher, **Thomas C. Hansard and Luke Hansard** who became the compiler of Parliamentary Report of the House of Commons in 1812. From 1909 the staff of the House of Commons took over the recording of debates but the name **Hansard** remained and was officially adopted in 1943.

Importance of Hansard

The Hansard is a full and complete record of everything said and done in Parliament. Its importance lies in the fact that it is the storage of the image of the Legislature, a reflection of its stature measured by the standard and quality of its debates. While an Act of Parliament is the letter of the law passed by Parliament, the Hansard captures the spirit and intent of the law.

The Hansard is a historical document from which we can understand the roles played by successive legislatures in the political and socio-economic development of the country. It will tell us the reasons why certain crucial legislative decisions (such as the Preventive Detention Act, PDA) and resolutions were taken. In this way, lessons may be learnt from the past. The electorate is able to evaluate the performance and effectiveness of the elected representatives through their contributions to debates.

The Hansard may capture the prevailing atmosphere and mood of the House by insertions such as "**uproar**" "**interruption**" "**hear, hear**" (not **yea yea**) all of which sometimes enliven debates. Hansard may therefore be described as the "**Mirror of Parliament**"

Recording, Production and Form of The Hansard

The Hansard is produced on a daily basis when the House is sitting and it will contain not only the debates but also all matters including Bills, Questions, Statements and Divisions taken in the House.

At the end of each Meeting of Parliament a bound volume consisting of all the daily Hansard is produced by the Editor. Editing of the bound volume includes indexes and lists of Ministers, Principal Officers and Staff of the House.

The Hansard is supplied to Members the following day after a sitting. It is available to the public for sale. ForeignParliaments are supplied with bound volumes on a reciprocal basis.

Correction of Speeches by Ministers and Members

The transcripts may be amended in respect of grammar and spelling at the instance of a Member but corrections of substance are not allowed.

Repetitions and redundancies are omitted without adding or altering the meaning of a speech.

Undelivered speeches cannot be inserted into the Hansard.

Unparliamentary expressions or language can only be expunged from the Hansard by the Speaker.

Hansard Department

Official Report or Hansard is a separate department which forms part of the Service under the Clerk's Department. The head of the Hansard Department is the Editor of Debates assisted by a Deputy and Assistant Editors of varying ranks.

The department is responsible for recording verbatim all speeches made in the House and in Standing Committees such as the Public Accounts Committee and the Committee of Privileges.

Hansard staff have rare skills. They possess high-speed shorthand skills that they acquire through systematic training. When covering proceedings, they usually work in relay teams of two or three persons for 10 or 15 minutes and another set takes over. At the conclusion of debates all but the last team would have finished their transcripts for editing by the Editor and his assistants for printing.

THE CHAMBER OF PARLIAMENT

In the House of Commons the Speaker's Chair stands in the East. Immediately below it is the Clerk's Table. And formerly, the Speaker had neither a desk nor a gavel.

Sets of benches for Members are arranged in the North and South, the two sets facing each other. The terms "front benchers" and "backbenchers" derived from these benches. Our Parliament used to follow the Westminster pattern of seating from 1957 to 1960. When it was decided that Ghana should become a republic a horse-shoe arrangement was suggested. The idea was that we should move away from the concept of Government and Opposition in favour of a consensus of Majority and Minority in accordance with our traditional methods of seeking agreement on controversial issues. The former terms somehow carried some acerbity with them and the parallel arrangement of seats conjured up a rather beligerent atmosphere. The horse-shoe arrangement of seating was in place for Republic Day in 1960 and the air was then filled with sounds of Majority and Minority. The Chamber of the old Parliament House could seat one hundred and forty Members.

It was felt that the horse-shoe was benign and engendered togetherness in diversity. In the present Chamber the Speaker's Chair stands in the East, with the Clerk's Table below it. The Chair is provided with a desk and a gavel. The new Chamber can seat two hundred Members.

Seating for Members also takes a horse-shoe form, except that the heel is more obtuse than in a horse-shoe. Like as of old, the majority sit in the South, to the right of the Speaker and the Minority in the North. Members can spill over either way.

Despatch box

In front of the Clerk's desk stands a table on which are placed two despatch boxes from which Ministers may speak. This custom took its rise from the early days at Westminster when important Ministerial papers were secured in a despatch box which was carried to the House. A Minister wishing to speak could place his box on the Table and speak from it.

PRESIDENT OF GHANA

The President of Ghana is the Head of State and Head of Government and the Commander-in-Chief of the Armed Forces.[39]

As an executive President, the President takes precedence over all other persons in Ghana.[40] He represents the majesty of the State and the dignity of his office must therefore be protected. As a result legal action should not be taken against him in the performance of his functions whilst he is in office.[41]

The President assumes office at the moment at which he takes and subscribes the Oath of Allegiance and the Presidential Oath by virtue of clause (3) of article 57 of the Constitution.

Term of office

The President is elected to hold office for a term of four years and is eligible to be elected for another term. In other words, he is only eligible to be elected to hold office for two terms, in terms of article 66 of the Constitution.

Election of President

The election of the President is by universal adult suffrage and is governed by article 63 of the Constitution. A presidential candidate must be a citizen of Ghana, having attained the age of forty years.

The nomination of a candidate for presidential election must be supported by a document signed by the candidate himself and by not less than two persons who are registered voters resident in the area of authority of each district assembly. The signed document must be delivered to the Electoral Commission on or before the day appointed as nomination day for the election. The presidential candidate must designate a person to serve as Vice-President.

Declaration of election result

A presidential candidate would not be declared elected unless he has obtained more than fifty percent of the votes of the total number of valid votes cast at the election.

Executive authority

The President is vested with full control over the Government and all executive acts of Government are taken in his name under article 58 of

---

39. *Clause (1) article 57 of the Constitution*
40. *Clause (2) article 57 of the Constitution*
41. *Clause (5) article 57 of the Constitution*

the Constitution. The executive power includes the formulation and implementation of development policies especially in the social and economic fields, initiation of legislation and making appointments in the executive sphere.

Vice-President
The Office of the Vice-President is governed by article 60 of the Constitution. The President may also assign to him other functions. Whenever the President dies, resigns or is removed from office, the Vice-President assumes the office of the President. In the absence of the President from the country or when he is incapacitated, the Vice-President is required to perform the functions of the President until he returns or is able to perform his functions.

In the absence of both the President and Vice-President from the country, the Speaker of Parliament is required to perform the functions of the President.

Oath of Vice-President
The Vice-President assumes office when he has taken and subscribed the Oath Of Allegiance and the Vice-Presidential Oath.

Attendance of Parliament
Although the Vice-President is not a Member of Parliament, he may attend the Sittings of Parliament and participate in the proceedings without the right to vote or to hold office in Parliament: (article 111 of the Constitution.)

MINISTERS OF GHANA
Article 76 of the Constitution provides for a Cabinet consisting of the President, the Vice-President and not less than ten and not more than nineteen Ministers of State. The Cabinet is to assist the President in the determination of the general policy of the Government. The President presides over Cabinet meetings and in his absence the Vice-President presides.

Ministers of State
The President is also required by article 78 of the Constitution to appoint Ministers of State from among Members of Parliament or persons qualified to be elected as Members of Parliament with the prior approval of Parliament. The majority of Ministers must be appointed from among Members of Parliament. The Ministers are to assist the

President in the exercise of his executive power and to take charge under his direction of departments he may assign to them for efficient running of the State.

Revocation of appointment and retirement
The President has power to revoke the appointment of Ministers if a vote of censure has been passed against him by Parliament or if the President is not satisfied with his performance or if the Minister is elected Speaker or Deputy Speaker or if he resigns or dies: article 81 of the Constitution.

The office of a Minister also becomes vacant immediately before the assumption of office by the President. In other words, all Ministers are deemed to have retired from office when the term of office of the President expires.

Emolumens of President, Vice-President and Ministers
The emoluments payable to the President, the Vice President and Ministers of State are determined under article 71 of the Constitution by Parliament on the recommendations of a Committee appointed by the President, acting in accordance with the advice of the Council of State.

MEMBERS OF PARLIAMENT

Elections before dissolution of Parliament
The Constitution requires that elections to Parliament must be held every four years. Usually the dissolution of Parliament precedes parliamentary elections. However, in our situation the Constitution demands that Parliament must complete its full statutory life of four years[42] and elections must be held at least one month before the dissolution.

Qualification
A person seeking to be elected a Member of Parliament must be a Ghanaian, must owe allegiance to Ghana only and must have attained the age of twenty-one years.[43] However, one can vote at the age of eighteen years.[44] A parliamentary candidate must also be a registered voter and resident in the constituency he wants to represent or hails from that constituency.

---

42. *Article 113 of the Constitution*
43. *Article 94 of the Constitution*
44. *Article 42 of the Constitution*

Eligibility

Eligibility for election to Parliament is based on two principles: (a) moral standing of the individual in the society and (b) natural incompatibility of a person's occupation with membership in the House. In the former case, a person adjudged bankrupt, or incompetent to hold public office by a report of a Commission or Committee of Inquiry, a lunatic or a person declared to be of unsound mind cannot be elected a Member of Parliament. In the latter category, persons holding certain jobs, for example, in the Police Service, Judicial Service and Civil Services are not eligible to be Members of Parliament. A Chief is also debarred from being elected to Parliament.[45]

Nomination of candidate

Nomination of a candidate for election to Parliament is determined by organised political parties except that individuals may stand as independent candidates. Usually a candidate is either chosen by party leaders in a constituency and approved by the national headquarters or imposed by the national executive council. A sitting Member is not automatically chosen as the candidate in a subsequent election if his chances of winning are slim or his performance in the House falls below expectation.

Loss of seats

The circumstances in which a Member loses his seat include absence from fifteen sittings of a Meeting of Parliament without permission in writing of the Speaker and is unable to offer reasonable explanation to the Committee of Privileges, or if he is expelled or resigns from Parliament, or if he leaves the party of which he was a Member at the time of his election to Parliament to join another party. If he is elected Speaker his seat becomes vacant, and upon the dissolution of Parliament he loses his membership of Parliament.

Emoluments

The emoluments payable to Members of Parliament are determined by the President on the recommendation of a Committee appointed by the President acting in accordance with the advice of the Council of State. The emoluments or salaries include allowances, facilities and privileges and retiring benefits or awards.

---

45. See generally articles 94 and 97 of the Constitution

PARLIAMENTARY STRUCTURES
To gain an insight into how our Parliament works, the roles of the key officers who make the institution function must be recognised.

The Parliamentary Service is structured as follows:
(a) The Office of the Speaker assisted by two Deputy Speakers;
(b) The House departments which constitute the Service of Parliament;
   (j) The Clerk's Department,
   (ii) The Marshal's Department,
   (iii) The Hansard Department,
   (iv) The Library and Research/Information Department,
   (v) Parliamentary Draftsman's Department (yet to be established),
   (vi) Administration and Finance Department,
   (vii) The Catering Department..

PRINCIPAL OFFICERS OF PARLIAMENT

Speaker
The most important officer in Parliament is the Speaker. He is one of three great officers of state and he ranks third in the official order of precedence after the President and the Vice-President The Speaker is the spokesman and representative of the House and the Protector of its Privileges and the Rights of Minorities. He may be elected from among the Members or from outside the Parliament.

The Speaker is both master and servant of the House. As master he has the power to preside over and control debates and the conduct of Members in the Chamber. He does not take part in debates and does not have a vote. His rulings cannot be challenged except upon a substantive motion.

Essential quality of Speaker
An essential quality of the Speaker is his absolute impartiality in the Chair where his role is one of a non- partisan referee. If he is a member of a party he should upon election sever all connections with his party and be seen to have done so. One of the qualities of a Speaker is that he must have endless patience to tolerate all Members and ensure that all points of view are expressed in the House. In carrying out his duties, he acts in accordance with the powers given him by the Constitution, by the Standing Orders, and by the House. In this sense he is the servant of the House. The Speaker's powers are therefore derived and not inherent.

Administrative role

The Speaker also has an administrative role. He is the chairman of the Parliamentary Service Board and has the over-all responsibility in the administration and management of the Service.[46]

Removal

The Speaker is removable from office upon a motion expressing "no confidence" in him, which is supported by at least three quarters of the total number of Members. If before the expiry of his term of office the Speaker dies or retires or is removed the House elects a new Speaker at its next Sitting.

Emoluments

The emoluments payable to the Speaker are determined by the President on the recommendations of a Committee appointed by the President acting in accordance with the Council of State.

Deputy Speaker

The Speaker is assisted by the First Deputy Speaker and the Second Deputy Speaker, one of whom must be elected from the Minority side.[47] During the unavoidable absence of the Speaker from the House the First Deputy Speaker presides over the debates and in the absence of the First Deputy, the Second Deputy takes over.

Clerk

The Clerk to Parliament is a public officer. Neither the Clerk nor his staff are civil servants. The Clerk is the principal adviser to the Speaker on the privileges, practice and procedure of Parliament. He is also consulted by Members of Parliament on procedural matters. As adviser on procedural matters, the Clerk must have a thorough understanding of the rules, procedures and practices of Parliament. This requires a constant and thorough training over the years. The work culture of Parliament is quite distinct from other services. It needs prompt attention to duty, efficient and courteous service to all Members.

The Clerk makes the arrangements for the Sittings of the House, prepares the Order Paper – the daily business arranged for the Sitting, keeps its records and engrosses it Bills. Bills passed by the House are authenticated by the Clerk for Presidential assent. One of the Clerk's

46. *Article 95 of the Constitution*
47. *Article 95 of the Constitution*

unenviable duties in our Parliament is to preside over the first Sitting of the newly elected Parliament for the purpose of the election of a new Speaker.

Clerk's political neutrality

As servant of the House, the Clerk has to demonstrate political neutrality in a multi-party parliamentary democracy and to ensure the impartial performance of his functions. Betrayal of these qualities may undermine the integrity, effectiveness and efficiency of the institution. It has been said that the Clerk and his staff live in the thick of politics yet they are apolitical. He is expected to provide strictly factual information and observe objectivity. In the heat of debate when tempers rise, he is to assist the Speaker to arbitrate between the ruling party and the minority party or parties. He works behind the scenes and in anonymity.

Head of Management Committee

The Clerk is the head of the Parliamentary Service and its accounting officer. He is also a member of the Parliamentary Service Board of which the chairman is the Speaker. The Clerk presides over the Management Committee comprising heads of department – the Clerk's Department, the Marshal's Department, the Hansard Department, the Administrative Department, the Library (Research and Information) Department and Catering Department.

Deputy-Clerk, Clerks-at-the-Table

The Clerk is assisted by the three Clerks-at-the-Table one of whom must be a Deputy Clerk. The designation Clerks-at-the-Table derives from the Clerk's Table in the Chamber in front of the Speaker's Chair. It is upon the Table that Papers are laid and notices of business may be placed during a Sitting. It has been said that Parliament cannot function without the Speaker or the Clerk who together constitute the king-pin.

The Hansard

The Hansard is the Official Report of the proceedings of Parliament. It is as nearly as possible verbatim. 'Hansard' was adopted as the name of the official report of Commonwealth Parliaments from the name Thomas Curtzan Hansard who became the compiler of the Parliamentary Report of the House of Commons from the year 1812.

Editor of Debates
The department is headed by the Editor of Debates. He is assisted by Assistant Editors and Verbatim Reporters of Debates. The Hansard is in two parts – The Daily Part and the Bound Volume. The Daily Part contains the Proceedings of each Sitting of Parliament. The Bound Volume consists of all the Daily Parts produced during each Meeting of Parliament.

THE PARLIAMENTARY SERVICE BOARD

Appointing Authority
The Parliamentary Service was established in accordance with article 124 of the Constitution and operates under the Parliamentary Service Act, (Act 460). The Service is controlled by a Board consisting of the Speaker as chairman, the Majority and the Minority Leaders and two other Members appointed on the recommendation of a Committee of the House. The Clerk of Parliament is also a member. The appointment of the Clerk and the other members of his staff is made by the Parliamentary Service Board in consultation with the Public Services Commission.

The Board has the duty to ensure effective and efficient administration of the Service. It determines conditions of service of staff and enforces discipline.

The Office of Majority and Minority Leaders
Both the Majority and Minority Leaders have office in Parliament. Non-elected Ministers do not hold office in Parliament. The two office holders, Majority and Minority Leaders are assisted by a Deputy Majority Leader and a Deputy Minority Leader and their Chief Whips. Both Leaders constitute the leadership of the House with whom the Speaker must consult on the business of the House and other important issues. They are usually the first to catch the Speaker's eye if they want to speak during important debates.

The Whips
The Chief Whips have office in Parliament and they provide important contacts between the party leadership and back-benchers of the same party. They usually keep Members informed about important business to be taken each week, indicating when their attendance is required on vital issues (a three-line whip) when a division is expected (a two-line whip) and when ordinary attendance is requested (a one-line whip).

PARLIAMENTARY TERMINOLOGY

Acquaintance with and knowledge of a few important terms that are used in parliamentary proceedings is essential to understand the nature and workings of Parliament.

A Member *puts a question*, when the Member asks a Question orally in the House at Question Time.

A Member *tables a motion* when the Member gives written notice of it which the Member has originally placed on the Clerk's Table.

A Member *moves* (or *makes*) or (*proposes*) a motion, when the Member presents it orally in the House.

A Member *speaks to the question*, by making a relevant contribution to the motion proposed.

The Speaker *proposes the question*, when the Speaker gives the House possession of a motion after it has been seconded. A motion would not be debated or amended or voted upon until the question has been proposed.

The Speaker *puts the question*, when the debate is over and the Speaker is going to ask for a decision.

The House *votes*, when it decides a question by the voices of Aye and No.

The House *divides*, when it decides a question by Members going through the division lobbies on a division.

The House is *counted out* when the absence of a quorum is brought to the notice of the Chair. If a quorum is not constituted within ten minutes of the giving of a direction to summon Members, the Speaker then adjourns the Sitting.

A Member is *named*, when the Speaker declares in the House that the Member has been guilty of some irregular or improper conduct especially for disregarding the authority of the Chair. The Member's personal name instead of his electoral constituency is called by the Speaker. The Member may then be suspended from the rest of the Sitting.

Sub-judice convention – is a convention that requires Members to refrain from making reference to certain matters pending before the courts.

Adjournment *sine die* - means that the House adjourns a Sitting indefinitely or without fixing a date for its next Sitting at the conclusion of a Meeting or a Session.

Reasoned amendment - is an amendment giving specific reasons for opposing the second or third reading of a Bill.

Maiden Speech - is the first speech made by a new Member in the House. The Speaker normally gives preference to the Member who may read from his notes on this occasion.

A Bill is read **the** *first time.*
A Bill is read **a** *second time.*
A Bill is read **the** *third time.*
A motion (or amendment) *is agreed to.*
A motion (or amendment) *is negatived.*
A clause in a Bill *is disagreed to.*
A Member *moves* the Second (or Third) Reading of a Bill.
A Bill is *passed* (not passed into law) upon its Third Reading.
A Bill is introduced or passed upon (not under) Certificate of Urgency.
The Minister of Finance *makes* the Budget Statement (not Budget Speech).

dilatory motion:	A member moves a dilatory motion when he intends to *delay* consideration of the question before the House. A motion to adjourn the debate or adjourn the House are devices to avoid decision taking. For example, a member may move "that the *debate* be now adjourned".
closure (motion):	A procedure *preventing* further adjournment of debate on a motion or on any stage of a bill. Closure of motion is intended to avoid delay in taking a vote on a motion at the end of the sitting. For example, a member may move "that the *question* be now put".

Appendix

GHANA'S LIVELY LEGISLATURE[48]

How Parliamentary Democracy has evolved

By S. N. Darkwa Former Clerk of Parliament

Since Ghana moved to a system of parliamentary democracy, the Parliament has steadily evolved into a unique and lively Legislature. It continues to change as it faces new procedural questions and challenges.

The hallmark of a vibrant and effective Parliament is its capacity to scrutinize government activities and to hold it to account. It has often been said that the price of multiparty democracy is eternal scrutiny. How have various parliaments performed under different constitutions of Ghana?

From one-party state

The 1964 constitution of the First Republic of Ghana gave the country a one-party state and a Parliament that was widely seen as subdued and compliant. The legislative powers conferred on the first President were enormous and parliamentary control over executive actions was virtually non-existent or ineffective.

While few Members found courage to give utterance to their views, many were wont to give unsolicited adulation to the President, on whom one Member moved a motion to confer life-presidency. However, the President did not accept the proposal which would have taken away the right of the people to exercise their franchise.

To parliamentary democracy

In sharp contrast, the 1969 constitution of the Second Republic provided for a multiparty parliamentary democracy. Parliament was vibrant and became the focal point of the electorate's desire for a good governance.

---

48. *[This article was originally published in the July 1999 issue of **The Parliamentarian** – Journal of the Parliaments of the Commonwealth]*

Having experienced a Parliament in a one-party state and military governments, in 1992 the constitution was changed and parliamentary democracy was now firmly chosen as the best option for the nation. Article 3 of the constitution of the Fourth Republic and the two constitutions before it had made it virtually impossible to introduce a motion in Parliament for the establishment of a one-party state in Ghana.

A forum for public debate

While the one-party state Parliament was reluctant to raise matters that could embarrass the executive, the multiparty Parliaments of the subsequent republics demonstrated a capacity to discuss all matters, big or small. Parliament has since been the forum where high-profile matters of state have been debated.

There were no opposition Members in the First Parliament of the Fourth Republic as a result of the opposition's boycott of the parliamentary election. The presence of the opposition in the Second Parliament increased the weight of public expectation of a vibrant Parliament. This Parliament has lived up to this expectation. The minority group has challenged government policies, taken the government to the Supreme Court over the President's nominees for ministerial appointments and generated sufficient publicity for its own cause to ensure that the government is accountable to the electorate.

The constitution of Ghana guarantees adequate privileges and immunities for Members to exercise their legislative and other roles in Parliament without fear or favour. The Chamber of the House, therefore, provides an opportunity for the opposition to confront the government on issues which it feels ought to be debated.

No debate can take place in Parliament without a Member first moving a motion. Every motion is intended to elicit a decision in the affirmative or negative. Moreover, matters chosen by the opposition are not only intended to generate publicity to enhance its own alternative programme or policy but also to force the government into the open.

Debate in Parliament may therefore be described as a confrontation between the opposition and government. While military and dictatorial governments would prefer secrecy and concealment of their actions, a vibrant opposition in a multiparty democracy would demand full disclosure of every government action.

An urgent motion

Local press and other media, quoting a Nigerian newspaper about an improper payment of money to the President of Ghana by the late

General Sani Abacha, then President of Nigeria, provided an opportunity for the opposition to force the government into the open.

The opposition Spokesman on Foreign Affairs, Hon. Hackman Owusu-Agyeman, MP, tabled a motion that sought to establish the truth or otherwise of the allegation.

The motion stated:
"That this House views with concern the recent allegations in the press and media of improper payment to the President by the government of the late General Abacha of Nigeria, which allegations have found their way on to the Internet and international press.

"That considering the seriousness of the allegations, which seek to bring the high office of the President into disrepute, the House take steps to safeguard the integrity of the presidency and the image of the country by requesting the government to set up a high-powered independent board of inquiry to determine the veracity of the allegation."

Almost one month passed without a decision regarding the admissibility or otherwise of the urgent motion. Mr. Owusu-Agyemang (who had established a reputation for raising urgent matters in the House; he was the Member who raised an urgent question soon after the first sitting of the new Parliament on why a Libyan aircraft was permitted to land in Ghana in violation of a UN Security Council Resolution) called the attention of the Speaker to ascertain the fate of the motion.

Mr. Speaker's ruling
On 10 December 1998, the Speaker, Rt Hon. Justice D.F. Annan, made his ruling in respect of the motion. He ruled:

I have had a certain amount of difficulty in coming to a decision whether or not to admit this motion. On the one hand I did not want to deny any Member or party in this House the opportunity to be heard in the House and to call for action on a matter that ought to be debated in the House. On the other hand, having regard to this particular proposal and the course of action envisaged therein, I have felt the need to satisfy myself that this is a proper case to be admitted for debate on the Floor of the House. I have in this respect guarded against making any judgement on the merits of the matter. Such a judgement falls exclusively within the authority of the House.

"In considering whether or not to admit this motion, I have observed that the reports being relied on to activate proceedings by way of motion, namely newspaper reports, amount in my opinion at the present time, to little better than rumours, having regard to the paucity of material evidence of any weight offered in support of, or to lend some credence to these media reports. I take the position that in all the circumstances and having regard to what information is available, as at now, in the public domain, to debate this motion at the present time would offer some credibility to a matter that on the stated facts, would seem to amount to nothing more than speculative reporting."

"This motion could constitute a precedent for starting a debate in the House in the absence of a credible basis for invoking the authority of the House. I would like to observe that House procedures other than by way of a motion would offer more appropriate responses at this point in time for the purpose of addressing the concerns which no doubt inform the request to set up an inquiry into these allegations. I, accordingly, rule that no proper foundation has been laid by the proponents of this motion to enable them to pursue the course of action contemplated in the motion and they can therefore not proceed with it until such time as more material become available to justify the course of action proposed therein."

The ruling is challenged
Barely 24 hours after the ruling, Mr. Owusu-Agyemang submitted a substantive motion to challenge the Speaker's ruling in accordance with Standing Order 78.

The motion read:
"That this House urges the Rt Hon. Speaker to review his decision not to admit the urgent motion on setting up a board of inquiry to look into the allegation of improper payment to the President by the government of former Nigerian Head of State, General Abacha, which urgent motion was originally submitted in my capacity as the Hon. Member of Parliament for New Juaben and minority spokesman for Foreign Affairs.

Mr Owusu-Agyemang sought vigorously to move the motion soon after the ruling by the Speaker. Mr. Owusu-Agyemang said the motion was of such topical interest and of national importance that it was sufficiently urgent to justify an early debate.

An urgent problem

He further felt that the allegation was so serious it was urgent to confront it in order to establish the impeccable integrity of the President and to restore the image of the nation. He argued that the House is the only forum privileged to debate the high profile matter asking for the President to be investigated.

He accordingly called on the Speaker to allow the motion to be debated without notice in accordance with Standing Order 78 which states that unless any order otherwise provides, notice shall be given of any motion which it is proposed to make, with certain exceptions including:

"(k) any motion the urgency of which is admitted by Mr. Speaker."
Continuing, he said: "Mr. Speaker, we cannot fail the good people of this nation. The allegation keeps on surfacing; my bag is full of press reports, documents from the Internet ... and the longer we keep this thing hanging, the longer the allegation hurts the presidency and this nation. What is the majority afraid of?"

Time is found

In his ruling, the Speaker said that he had admitted the fresh urgent motion challenging his ruling on the original motion and that time must be found to debate it.

The government fiercely resisted the attempt to move the motion on that day without notice in accordance with Standing Order 98. A vote was taken to postpone debate to 15th December.

Government supporters felt that the opposition was merely reverting to type, and that it saw an opportunity to unnerve the government and generate unwarranted publicity. But the opposition would not let the matter be swept under the carpet.

The debate is aborted

The House missed a rare opportunity to debate fully for the first time in the history of Ghana's Parliament a high-profile motion that raised fundamental procedural matters. The resolution of the procedural difficulties would have served as a precedent to guide the House in future. Full participation in debate by both opposition and government was aborted following the opposition walk-out over the behaviour of a Deputy Minister of Agriculture against whom a complaint of a breach of privilege was made without the matter being referred to the Committee of Privileges.

Procedural issues raised

The mover of the Motion, Hon. Owusu-Agyemang, and the seconder of the Motion, Hon. Nana Akufo-Addo, opposition Spokesman on Legal and Constitutional Affairs, as well as Hon. Kwamena Ahwoi, Minister for Local Government and Rural Development, raised relevant procedural issues which should have been settled once and for all.

The thrust of Mr. Owusu-Agyemang's argument was that one of the grounds on which Mr. Speaker based his ruling, namely that "reports being relied upon (for tabling the original urgent Motion) amounted to little better than rumours", was not sufficient to dismiss his Motion. He said the so-called rumours were worthy of investigation

In seconding the Motion, Mr. Akufo-Addo stated that it was not only the first time in the life of this Parliament that a formal written ruling had been given by the Speaker in exercise of his powers under Standing Order 79 (4), it was also the first time that the House was reviewing the Speaker's ruling. Standing Order 79 (4) states that "Every notice (of a Motion) shall be submitted to Mr. Speaker who shall direct that it be printed in its original terms or with such amendments as he shall direct, or that it be returned to the Member who submitted it as inadmissible".

Speaker's powers not absolute

He argued that Standing Order 79 (4) does not confer absolute power on the Speaker to refuse any Motion that shall be submitted to him.

The Speaker intervened to say that the fact that his ruling was being challenged was evidence of his restricted powers. The House could decide whether he was right or wrong.

Mr. Akuffo-Addo then gave a few examples of out of order Motions or occasions when Mr. Speaker can exercise his powers to refuse to admit. First, where the constitution has expressly prohibited Parliament to pass a law to alter an entrenched provision.

For example, Article 3 (1) of the constitution says that Parliament shall have no power to enact a law establishing a one-party state. A Motion for establishing a one-party state is therefore not a proper subject to be introduced for debate in Parliament.

Second, the Speaker shall refuse a Motion that seeks to pass retroactive legislation (Article 107 of the constitution).

Third, the Speaker may refuse a Motion where the language of the motion is improper, obscene, lewd, insulting or abusive. Such a Motion may be amended in such a manner as may be acceptable for debate.

He argued that apart from the out of order motions, the House can consider any matter of public interest which is not couched in language that is improper. He said, "my respectful argument, Mr. Speaker, is that you have no power to prevent such a Motion from being heard on the Floor of the House". He argued that the power to reject a motion on its merit resided in the House and not in the Speaker who could not participate in debates.

Mr. Speaker said" "It is not for the House to decide whether a Motion is to be admitted or not. It is the prerogative of the Speaker. The issue here is whether that power has been properly exercised or not, not that that power does not reside in the Speaker. If that power does not reside in the Speaker, then where does it reside?"

Drama in Parliament

While Mr. Akufo-Addo was advancing an argument against the power exercised by the Speaker in disallowing the original urgent Motion, the Minister of Local Government and Rural Development, Mr. Kwamena Ahwoi, rose on a point of order. The Minister had hardly raised his point of order when an opposition Member, Hon. Agyei-Acheampong, taunted him saying "are you a lawyer?" This remark provoked a Deputy Minister of Agriculture, Hon. Mike Acheampong, to anger that nearly led to physical confrontation with the opposition Member. Proceedings were halted for about seven minutes amidst uproar.

After calm had been restored, the Minority Leader, Hon. J. H. Mensah, raised a complaint of breach of privilege against the Deputy Minister for an alleged threat of violence on the Floor of the House.

The Speaker refused to refer the complaint to the Committee of Privileges. He said that he was not aware of any conduct of any Member of the House which deserved to be referred to the Committee. The Minority Leader and his group then walked out.

The smaller minority group remained in the House to continue to debate with the government.

Mr. Ahwoi, in his contribution, raised a relevant procedural matter. He was not clear whether the Motion was urging the House to review the Speaker's ruling or the Speaker was being asked to review his own ruling.

In his contribution, the Attorney-General and Minister of Justice, Dr. Obed Asamoah, said that he found himself unable to appreciate some of the legal arguments put forward by the opposition. He found no authority to support the view that the Speaker was not the last authority with regard to the admissibility or otherwise of motions.

The debate was concluded without the participation of the main opposition group which initiated it. When the question was put the motion was negatived.

Conclusions

Among the procedural issues raised are (I) whether the Speaker has absolute power to disallow any motion he considers inappropriate; (ii) whether the Speaker could preside over debate in which his ruling has been challenged and (iii) whether the Speaker should have referred the conduct of the Deputy Minister to the Committee of Privileges.

With regard to the power to admit or disallow the motion, the Speaker himself conceded that his power to admit or refuse motions that come before him is not absolute. The fact that his ruling can be challenged by substantive motion imposes limitations on his power. In fact, the constitution has carefully provided that no absolute power is concentrated in any one organ of state or in any office holder in the exercise of his functions. In the case of entrenched provisions of the constitution, Parliament is constrained from debating a motion that seeks to alter such provisions without going through the lengthy process of amending the constitution. These entrenched Articles in the constitution may be classified as improper subjects for debate in the House.

Out of order

There are also a few "out of order" Motions that may not be admitted for debate. Among them are Motions that are sub-judice and which are likely to prejudice the interest of parties in matters pending judicial decision or motions which anticipate a matter to be considered in the reasonably near future or Motions that are unduly long or Motions that are not couched in proper parliamentary language.

Apart from the above types of Motions, the bulk of competent opinion on parliamentary practice and procedure agree that "the main task of Parliament is to secure full discussion and ventilation of all matters in the House and that no issue is too big or too small for parliamentary consideration."

Another issue that has exercised the mind is whether the House could debate rumours or allegations that a Member considers worthy of investigation.

Rumours and allegations

It is generally accepted that allegations made in good faith are permissible but the Member making such allegations must first satisfy himself about the authenticity of his information. While it is agreed that unsubstantiated allegations may not be permitted in the House, the freedom to make allegations which a Member in good faith believes to be true or are at least worthy of investigation is regarded as fundamental. Were it not so, freedom of speech would be severely constrained if everything said has to be proved true before it was uttered.

Of course, frivolous rumours or allegations may be ignored or treated with, or beneath, contempt but where they impugn the integrity of another person steps should be taken to safeguard that person's reputation.

The Speaker presides

No Member raised the issue of propriety or otherwise of the Speaker presiding over a Motion challenging his own ruling. It is not normal for a Member to be present when a matter in which he is an interested party is being debated unless his presence is meant to provide him with an opportunity to defend himself. It is even more embarrassing for Speaker to preside over debate in which his ruling is challenged. Since he can neither vote nor participate in debate in accordance with Parliament's standing orders he should have been spared the job of presiding over the debate in which he was constantly prompted to intervene.

Hon. Kojo Armah, one of the few Members of the opposition who remained in the Chamber to continue the debate, summed up the feelings of his colleagues with regard to the conduct of the Deputy Minister.

He said "Mr. Speaker, I find it a little disheartening we have come to this point in the rather hearty debate... despite the heckling and the noise. I believe we were making headway. I find it rather unfortunate that the Deputy Minister who is not a Member [The constitution allows a non-elected Member who is a Minister to attend sittings and participate in debate without the right to vote] of this House should leave his seat and confront another Member of this House on the opposite side. Continuing, he said "heckling and interruptions have been part of the practice of this House but it was improper for a Deputy Minister to leave his seat and attempt to assault another Member". He felt that it would set a bad precedent if the House glossed over the incident.

Lively debate

Heckling enlivens debate. Debates in the Chamber are not expected to be heard in total silence. An innocuous aside or interruption, such as, "are you a lawyer?" should not provoke so much anger as to lead to physical confrontation. A Member's reaction or response to taunts can enhance or diminish his reputation.

Finally, the Speaker must enjoy the confidence of both sides of the House because trust in the Speaker is the key to getting business through in the House. The minority parties must be protected to ensure that their points of view are canvassed so that their frustrations do not find an outlet in walk-outs and press statements.

At the same time, the Speaker must ensure that the wishes of the majority party are not unduly frustrated by the minority abusing the rules of the House. The Speaker's role as the defender of the rights of Parliament and Members, is essential to preserve the integrity of a Legislature in a partisan political system. The independence, impartiality and authority of the Speaker must not only be seen and protected but should also be respected.

The House must strive to achieve a consensus on some major national issues. It is suggested that there should be consultations behind the scenes, with the Speaker exercising a moderating influence on the majority and minority sides, to resolve disputes before they come into the open.

Bibliography

Ayensu/Darkwa – *Evolution of Parliament in Ghana* (Accra: Assembly Press 1999)

Commonwealth Parliamentary Association – *Guidelines for Training of Parliamentary Staff.* (London: CPA 1996)

Derek Heater – *Parliament at work*

Erskine May (ed. Sir C. Boulton) *Parliamentary Practice, 21st Edition)* (London: Butterworths 1989)

JAC Griffith and Michael Ryle, *Parliament, Functions, Practice and Procedures* (London: Sweet and Maxwell 1989)

Kenneth Bradshaw and David Pring – *Parliament and Congress.* (London, Anchor Press 1981)

Paul Silk – *How Parliament works*(Longman, London and New York 1989)

Philip Laundy – *Parliament and People* (Ashgate, Aldershot, Brookfield USA, Singapore, Sydney 1997)

Standing Orders of Parliament of Ghana (Accra: Assemblies of God Press 1995)

The 1992 Constitution of the Republic of Ghana (Accra: Assembly Press: 1992)

Friedrich Naumann Foundation and Ghana Centre for Demotratic Development (CDD) – *Parliament and Democratic Governance in Ghana's Fourth Republic.* (Accra 2000)

Index

www.ingramcontent.com/pod-product-compliance
Lightning Source LLC
Chambersburg PA
CBHW071138280326
41935CB00010B/1280